Resources
Rock

*Buy Lo
Sell Hi*

Resources
Rock

How to Invest in and Profit from the
Next Global Boom in Natural Resources

Malvin Spooner
with Pamela Clarke

INSOMNIAC PRESS

National Library of Canada Cataloguing in Publication Data

Spooner, Malvin, 1955-
    Resources rock: profiting from the next global boom in natural resources / Malvin Spooner with Pamela Clarke.

Includes index.
ISBN 1-894663-62-4

1. Natural resources. 2. Investments. 3. Finance, Personal.
I. Clarke, Pamela, 1963- II. Title.

HC85.S66 2004   332.67'8   C2003-907476-5

The publisher gratefully acknowledges the support of the Canada Council, the Ontario Arts Council and the Department of Canadian Heritage through the Book Publishing Industry Development Program. We acknowledge the support of the Government of Ontario through the Ontario Media Development Corporation's Ontario Book Initiative.

Printed and bound in Canada

Insomniac Press
192 Spadina Avenue, Suite 403
Toronto, Ontario, Canada, M5T 2C2
www.insomniacpress.com

THE CANADA COUNCIL | LE CONSEIL DES ARTS
FOR THE ARTS | DU CANADA
SINCE 1957 | DEPUIS 1957

ONTARIO ARTS COUNCIL
CONSEIL DES ARTS DE L'ONTARIO

DISCLAIMER

Please note that statements made in this book regarding a subjective projection, estimates, expectations or predictions may be forward-looking statements within the meaning of applicable securities laws and regulations. The authors and publisher caution that such statements involve risk and uncertainty, and that actual results may differ from those expressed or implied. While every effort was made to ensure that all information in this book was current and accurate at time of publication, the authors and publisher are not responsible for any errors that might have been made.

This book is dedicated to the professional explorers and developers whose ingenuity and brute determination provide the raw materials necessary for our civilization to progress.

TABLE OF CONTENTS

Introduction
Stop Singing the Blues, It's Time to Rock 11

Chapter One
The Next Global Boom 15

Chapter Two
The Canadian Resource Sector 29

Chapter Three
Diamonds 37

Chapter Four
Gold 49

Chapter Five
Base Metals 65

Chapter Six
Oil and Gas 79

Chapter Seven
Coal 91

Chapter Eight
Uranium 97

Chapter Nine
Paper and Forestry Products 101

Chapter Ten
Fertilizers 111

Chapter Eleven
Flow-Through Shares 119

Chapter Twelve
Evaluating Investment Opportunities 127

Chapter Thirteen
Some Key Players 141

Epilogue
Beyond 2004: Can the boom last? 193

Acknowledgements 199

Index 201

Introduction

Stop Singing the Blues, It's Time to Rock

The crash of the high-tech market in the spring of 2000 severely hurt investors and shocked advisors who never thought that the market could sink so low. During one of the lowest points after the crash, I was speaking with a veteran investment advisor who said: "I'd never buy resources, ever."

There couldn't have been a better indicator for me that it was time to begin investing in the resource sector. If one of the most influential people in the financial community was staunchly against something, then it was time to find out if the market was at (or near) its lowest point, and whether or not it was poised to rebound. It's one of the most basic premises of how to make money: buy low, sell high.

Of course, it's also a difficult thing to do when you're an investor. It takes a lot of courage to put your hard-earned money into a sector or even a single stock when nobody else is interested in it. And it takes even more courage to sell a winner. Simply put, that's true contrarian investing and I'm enjoying a successful career doing exactly that.

Contrarian investing amounts to doing the opposite of everyone else, based on an objective analysis of the facts at hand. In many ways, it's like playing in a band—you sometimes have to block out what the other musicians are doing so you can deliver your best performance.

It's also been my experience that the one stock people swear they would never buy ends up being one of the most profitable investments they ever could have made. Sort of like the market's Murphy's Law.

After listening to the well-known advisor staunchly refuse to buy resources, I did some extensive research and came to the conclusion that—after a twenty-year slump—it was time to start buying resources. I launched a mutual fund that held only resource-sector stocks shortly thereafter.

One year later, the return on the fund was 100.64%, a return that was unheard of in a market where the next best fund posted a one-year return of 38.8%. Hindsight is 20/20, but looking back, the advisor was essentially saying to me: "I'm not interested in taking a chance that could double my client's money."

However, he was right about one thing. The risk was huge. At the time, if you were an investment advisor recommending that your clients put their money in resources you risked being a pariah. In my business, your reputation is all you've got so most advisors aren't keen on losing it. Well, that was a risk I could live with and the investors who bought the fund were well-rewarded. In less than twelve months, my hunch paid off with a record return.

I say "hunch" but in fact it was much more than that. As a money manager, I have tracked the resource sector for more than twenty years so making the decision to launch a mutual fund that only invested in resource companies was based on years of experience, a thorough analysis of the sector, and a review of the current economic conditions around the world. All of the factors indicated that the time was right for the resource sector to take a position on center stage for the next few years, and provide investors with some chart-topping returns.

In this book, I'll address the key issues that will enable you to cash in on the next global boom in natural resources. I'll tell you why I believe 2004 is the best time to invest in resource companies. I'll also explain in everyday terms how investors can get a substantial, but largely unknown tax break from buying shares in the resource sector.

The timing has never been better for you to invest with confidence in the resources market. A wealth of information is available in a timely and accessible format thanks to the technology revolution. Also, countless software or Internet-based tools can facilitate the analysis of the vast amounts of data. It is possible for investors to empower themselves these days.

While I won't be covering the high-tech tools that are available (there are many others who are more knowledgeable about that subject), I will ensure that once you've read this book, you will be able to make resource sector decisions from a well-informed position. Working with this knowledge, you can then choose to work on your own or draw on the experience of your investment advisor to profit from natural resources.

My goal in writing *Resources Rock* is to explain in a straightforward manner how to understand the frequently maligned resources sector and how to invest in diamonds, gold, metals, oil and gas, coal, uranium, forestry or fertilizer sub-sectors. This is not meant to be the definitive guide to resources, but rather a pragmatic introduction to the sector and its cycles. I deliberately kept the explanations as simple as possible—not to insult experienced investors reading this book, but to remove the mystique about how economies function, how companies make money, and to show how anyone with basic knowledge and common sense can become a shrewd investor.

Everyone who reads *Resources Rock* will be in a position to evaluate resource sector shares, figure out which companies are the Real McCoys, and which ones are just stock promoters with slick brochures. After nearly two decades of declining stock prices, resources are poised to hit record highs. The time is right to truly understand, and profit from, the resource sector.

Malvin Spooner

CHAPTER ONE
The Next Global Boom

Think back—way back for some of us—to your first high-school dance. Maybe the DJ played your favorite song, your partner was an incredible slow dancer, and you made plans to go out on a future hot date. Or, maybe you spent the entire evening sitting on a bench, waiting for the moment when you'd be asked to dance instead of doing something to make it happen.

Investing in resources is a lot like that first dance. It can be nerve-wracking, stressful, but ultimately sweet if you're prepared to take some chances. Doing the research, then mustering the courage to make the investment can be as agonizing as that long, lonely walk across the dance floor. In both cases, you risk failure on a variety of fronts: you get turned down for the dance/the stock dives just after you buy it; your partner can't dance/the market plateaus; you start to sweat uncontrollably/you panic and sell your shares as soon as they go up or down by 5%.

Most people won't admit what went wrong if things don't work out as they had planned. They're quick to blame their friends or their advisor, or say the music or the market just wasn't right. While nothing can reverse your experience at your first dance, it is time to rethink investing in resources. Many factors, which will be explained in great detail in this chapter, indicate investors in the resource sector will eventually be dancing away with some record profits.

Why Now?

Well, it's not just in music that timing is everything. It's also the case when it comes to investing. For years, the average prices of shares in resource sector stocks—from gold to diamonds to forest products—were at record low levels. Fraught with scandals such as the infamous Bre-X debacle, battered by international trade disputes, and smeared with the long-standing reputation of being populated by fly-by-night companies, the resource sector has not been able to pull out of its widespread slump in more than twenty years.

Unfortunately, people usually only feel comfortable investing when everything appears to be just perfect. Before they make a move, they want prices for commodities such as gold, metals or forest products to be strong, and companies to be profitable and have backing from a robust economy. They're often sorely disappointed.

If investors jump into the market when all the signs are positive, then the real gains have already been made and there is little, if any, room for serious profits to be had. It's like asking someone to dance when they're swaying slowly in somebody else's arms. You're a little late. Likewise, when the market is hot, it's best to consider selling your shares, not buying them.

The ideal time for buying shares is just *before* all of the above factors are in place—before commodity prices are strong; before revenues are rising steadily; before the company makes a profit; and before the economy is back on its feet. Just like the best time to ask someone to dance is when they're sitting alone, looking seriously bored. Enough of the analogies. Let's address the most important timing factor of all: the industrial cycles of the resource sector.

Cyclical Industry

During the late 1980s and early 1990s, when Northern Telecom and American Barrick were performing fabulously both as businesses and as stock investments, the forest products industry was in the midst of one of its worse slumps ever. When it looked like things just couldn't get any worse for the sector, the time was right to begin buying stocks before the situation improved.

At the time, MacMillan Bloedel Ltd. was one of the largest publicly traded Canadian paper and forest products companies. Since everyone was talking about the horrific state of the economy in B.C.—and specifically about the sorry state of the forest products industry in the beleaguered province—it was difficult for investment advisors to recommend their clients buy shares in MacMillan Bloedel. If they did, they'd be challenged about the tough conditions in the industry and more than likely, their professional abilities would be questioned.

Wise advisors would retort, politely of course, that the rough markets and the wretched state of the market is why the stock was so cheap. As it was, people started buying shares in MacBlo several months later, paying a substantially higher price than if they had bought the shares when the earnings were at their lowest. While it is easier to invest in a company when their earnings are up and their future looks bright, at that point, the lion's share of the profits has already been made. It's then time to sell.

Later on, when the forest products sector had recovered, the president of MacBlo gave an update to investors in Toronto about the company's financial forecast and strategic plans. He predicted steadily rising revenues, cash flow and earnings for the next several years, and then detailed how they'd be spending the windfall on building new mills and making improvements to existing ones.

This is one of the many cases where senior management had forgotten altogether that they work in a cyclical industry not a growth industry. It was definitely time to sell every stock you owned in the forest products industry and wait for the next buying opportunity— even though it might not occur for years. As mentioned before, the best time to buy shares is when the market seems to be the bleakest. Buy the stock when the company is losing a lot of money, and sell the shares when they're making more money than ever before.

Selling at the Top
It sounds simple to sell the shares when they're at the top of the market, but it's much harder to do than it appears. After all, unless

you own a crystal ball, how can you figure out when it's the top and when it's the bottom of the market? You can't exactly, but it is possible to read the signs and buy when it's at or close to the bottom, and sell when it's at or close to the top of the market. Only by looking back will you know if your timing was bang on.

If you can muster up the courage to do this (the hardest part is selling when the company is making strong gains), you can make good money in resource stocks, and will likely avoid the pitfalls. The best news of all is that because resource commodities are cyclical, you can repeat this process over and over—until you're rich, or at the very least, richer.

The key is to do your own research with your eyes wide open. You can't afford to listen to research analysts or believe everything that the executives at resources companies have to say. First of all, it's only natural that companies will want to show off their operations when things are going well. Conversely, they'll want to keep a low profile when the market is giving them a real beating.

For example, during the last bull market for gold, senior managers at one company boasted about hiring several business development professionals to find acquisition candidates as a means of fueling their growth. Shortly thereafter, the bottom fell out of the gold price. That meant even the most superior gold deposits and mining operations with the best track records were available for virtually pennies.

So what did the acquisition team do? Absolutely nothing. Why? Because it's infinitely easier to explain to a board of directors why you're buying a company during good times—even if the price is significantly more than what they would have paid a few years (or even in some cases just a few months) earlier. It's virtually impossible for the same people to support the purchase of an outstanding asset at a rock-bottom price when the market is in a slump with no end in sight.

Promotes and Scams

The biggest hurdle for people interested in investing in resources is that the sector has long been viewed as being on the sleazy side of the investment scale, a reputation that has been enhanced by the abundance of "promotes" in the sector. A "promote" is a group of fly-by-nighters who create a company, buy some moose pasture in the middle of nowhere, and then work hard to encourage people to invest in "the next great gold mine." They cash out and disappear long before the hapless investors see any returns.

Unfortunately, such scams are as prevalent today as they were during the Klondike Gold Rush in the 1890s, although securities regulators have made it more difficult for them to flourish. The most recent example, and by all standards, the most remarkable because it got out of control, is Bre-X Minerals. While Bre-X may have been the most notorious scandal, it was hardly the only mining investment disaster. Bre-X and its counterparts are incredibly valuable reminders of what not to do when investing in resources: "Don't buy what you don't understand" and "Do your research."

Another major reason why people tend to shy away from investing in resources is simply because they're human. Even those who are well-educated about how the resource sector works are still affected by public sentiment. Of the thousands of investment advisors, only a handful are comfortable investing in resources, even though the majority enjoy discussing what's hot and what's not in the sector. This is hardly surprising.

Buying at the Bottom
First of all, it's a long shot to find someone who is willing to shrug off conventional wisdom and buy a commodity when it's at the bottom of the market. Not many advisors were keen to recommend buying gold stocks when the price of gold got down to $250 per ounce. Much of the downward pressure on the price of gold bullion was due to open market sales by leading central banks. It was a spiral. There wasn't much demand for gold at the time, so when a large supply hit the market, the price necessary to make the sale fell. The falling price inspired central banks (which only hold gold for investment reasons these days) to behave like inexperienced investors and sell more of it.

GOLD PRICE OVER 20 YEARS (fig. 1)

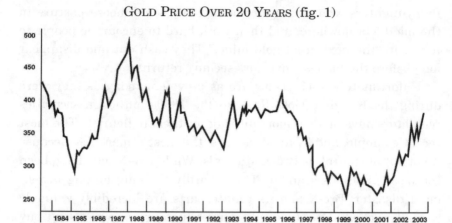

Reading the press reports at the time, you would have thought that the price was going to go so low that central banks in every country would sell gold in the open market indefinitely. Once this selling stopped, the price began a steady climb to current levels. Of course, now that the price is firmer, the central banks have lost all interest in selling gold. Even the world's leading brain trusts—and there's no shortage of financial gurus working for central banks—revert to the same foolhardy "buy high and sell low" patterns when it comes to investment decisions.

Second, it's an even longer shot to find advisors who are willing to take on the Herculean task of explaining to their clientele why they think it's a good time to buy a loser.

Understanding Cycles

A big problem is that a committee usually runs research departments in investment firms. Advisors rely on the proprietary research published by investment analysts, and the last thing investment analysts want to do (well, at least the ones who want to keep their jobs) is to recommend a sector that's in the dumpster. Despite the fact that researchers may readily admit "off the record" that the time is right to buy the stocks, peer pressure and political risk makes this admission untenable in a public forum.

How can researchers say to an army of investment advisors, "Hey, the commodity price is under extreme pressure due to a huge inventory overhang, demand for it is sucking wind, and the companies are all losing money. Therefore, I highly recommend that your clients buy it"? They can't say that. So when it comes to investing in resources, the advisors have to go it alone.

That's a shame. Although every resource (base metals, precious metals, forest products, petrochemicals and fertilizers) cycle is different and influenced by a plethora of variables, they all have one thing in common—the cycle. For example, there's the hog cycle: when prices for pork bellies skyrocket, farmers have more profits to reinvest so they produce more hogs. Then there's a surplus of the critters so prices of pork bellies begin to plummet. Farmers then aren't earning enough money to feed their hogs, so they cut back on production and another shortage ensues...and round and round it goes.

Most resource industries follow a similar pattern. When the market demand for a commodity is soft, prices fall and inventories rise. Companies aren't profitable enough to increase production (by exploring for new mineral deposits, looking for oil and gas wells, developing coal mines, building new pulp-and-paper mills, etc.) as long as inventories remain high and prices for the commodity are low. Then when demand for the resources picks up, inventories are reduced, sometimes quite rapidly depending upon the commodity. However, prices don't usually get higher until the inventory gets to the point where the threat of a chronic shortage is very real.

When it looks like a shortage is imminent, the price for the commodity rises, suppliers start to earn some profits once again, but it can take quite a long time before businesses can respond by increasing production. After a discovery, it can take seven to ten years to get a mine approved and built, which usually means missing a price cycle.

Environmental hurdles make the lead times even longer today than has been the case in the past. Take the forestry sector. If there was a shortage of lumber, then it used to be just a matter of harvesting more trees to meet the demand. Nowadays, many factors, mainly political and environmental ones, need to be considered before production can be increased. Even so, a cycle will always exist.

The Right Timing

The biggest challenge is to invest in resources at the right time in the cycle. All too often, the old saying "once burned, twice shy" is applicable when it comes to timing investments. The energy sector has many good examples of this conundrum. In the spring of 2003, the prospect of war in Iraq raised the possibility that there would be a shortage of oil. Such a prospect received a lot of press coverage, understandably so since it affects all of us. The price of a barrel of oil was rising rapidly then, so this is when most investors called their advisors and asked to be invested in the oil resource sector.

Bad move. This was one of the worst times to put money in oil and gas stocks. If investors had looked at some charts, they would have seen that energy prices and the stocks of oil and gas companies had been rising steadily up until that time. Demand worldwide had been strong in comparison to supply, and because suppliers were coming out of a rather long slump, they didn't have the capabilities to boost production as fast as demand was rising.

When U.S. and British forces invaded Iraq, global inventories for crude and natural gas were still low, and the high prices caused by the crisis had given the industry plenty of incentives to invest their capital to put their reserves into production. At the time of writing this book, energy sector stocks are owned by a variety of investors. Sadly, they are probably all wondering why their energy stocks have been declining in value despite the relatively high commodity prices and the record-breaking earnings announcements.

It's because the investors were too late. They bought the stocks too late in the energy sector cycle. If they had bought the same stocks when there was an excess supply of oil and gas, no Iraqi invasion on the horizon, and lousy commodity prices, they could sell them at this time for a huge profit.

Market Rebound

As their stocks spiral downward, investors usually sell them, and become soured on the whole business of investing in resource stocks. One bad experience often turns people off a particular sector for an extended period of time. How many investors were keen on buying high-tech stocks when Nortel Networks was trading below $1 in October of 2002?

A general rule of thumb is that there's almost always one resource sector outperforming the overall stock market. The trick is to identify it early, participate in the cyclical rebound, and then move along to the next boom—this is a formula for successful investing.

Unfortunately, the average investor's enthusiasm for stocks in the resource sector is directly linked to how well it's already performed. This is hazardous logic (not obvious to those who throw their hard-earned dollars at a losing proposition). In these cases, the odds of winning money are much better in Las Vegas.

Buying shares in resource companies at the peak of their cycle can only result in riding them down into the abyss of a cycle trough. If the average investor could be convinced (many investment advisors try and fail) to increase their commitment in the trough they'd be better off for it. Unfortunately, they'll wait until their stocks hit the absolute bottom and then they sell them in frustration.

So how do you know when it's time to invest and when it's time to sell? The first place to start is to take a good look at the big picture: the global economy. It's not as boring as most people assume. Just think of how much money you'll be making if you can wrap your mind around the fact that supply and demand are the main factors in choosing good investments.

Going back to our opening analogy, supply is like the number of guys at the high-school prom who really know how to dance, trying to meet the tremendous demand of the girls who want to dance with them. Because there is such a limited supply, the guys who can dance are more "valuable" than their buddies with two left feet.

China and India

To understand why it's such a good time to invest in resource stocks, you need to know that two of the fastest growing economies in the world are China and India. Though economically more advanced than other so-called developing economies, they need so many products and technologies that they'll be massive consumers of natural resources for many years to come.

PERCENTAGE CHANGE IN REAL GNP/GDP

Country	2001	2002
China	7.3%	8.0%
South Korea	3.0%	6.1%
India	4.2%	4.9%
Philippines	3.2%	4.6%
Russia	5.0%	4.3%
Canada	1.5%	3.4%
USA	0.3%	2.4%
Spain	2.7%	2.0%
UK	2.0%	1.6%
Germany	1.8%	1.2%
France	1.4%	0.8%
Italy	0.6%	0.4%
Japan	0.4%	0.3%
Switzerland	1.1%	0.1%

Source of Statistics: International Monetary Fund

For example, the majority of people in India or China don't have conventional telephones, let alone coaxial cable or fiber-optic broadband access. As they become more prosperous, they'll demand the same communications abilities that we take for granted. To meet this demand, companies will need a tremendous supply of raw resources—such as metals for wiring or constructing cable towers—to establish these networks.

Another important factor is that India and China both have an inexpensive, yet well-educated, labour force. This makes them extremely competitive in the global marketplace, and ensures their position as major suppliers of manufactured goods to the rest of the world. The problem is that they have a limited range, or don't have a steady supply of natural resources within their borders, so they need to import the raw materials in order to make the products.

Thanks to the huge gains in productivity made possible by recent technological and telecommunications innovations (that's one positive by-product of the tech bubble), the pace of growth in India and China is much quicker than in Europe or North America. The rapid rate of development is good news for resource suppliers as it means the developing countries can afford to buy the raw resources that they need to build new buildings, install new communication systems and produce new technology. Like other economic cycles, new infrastructure means they'll be able to manufacture more products, thereby increasing their exports, and earning more money to buy even more resources to make more goods.

At the same time that India and China are consuming raw materials sourced from Canada, Australia—and increasingly South America and Africa—their people want to buy goods and services such as entertainment, technology and fashion from Europe, Canada and the U.S. It's only human nature that they want to increase their standard of living. If they start buying products from our country, then our economy is given a good boost.

To meet the new demands for their products, manufacturers will have to buy raw materials to make the products. The catch is that they'll be competing with producers in developing countries for the same resources. This increased competition will drive up the prices that companies are willing to pay for natural resources. This is a sign that the global boom in resources is well underway, a boom that promises to produce gains that haven't been seen in this sector in years.

Tech Bubble
Timing is the key reason why this boom in natural resources is about to happen. Simply put, a variety of unpredictable and catastrophic world events have occurred in the last few years, all of which have set the stage for the coming boom in the resource sector. The technology market bubble was the real starting point.

On its own, the tech bubble wasn't such an unusual phenomenon as there have been so many other hot markets in the past. It does, however, stand out as being the first time that the U.S. federal government attempted to manage a market boom. The government's clumsy attempts at manipulating the market were disastrous and made the fallout after the bubble burst in the spring of 2000 worse than they ever could have anticipated.

When policy-makers hiked prime interest rates in 1999 to combat what Federal Reserve Chairman Alan Greenspan called "irrational exuberance," they made a huge error in judgment. The problem was that they failed to understand that the high-tech market frenzy was not an economic phenomenon. The "exuberance" was confined to the dot.com market, as the overall economy was not booming at all. By raising interest rates, which is a fundamental cost of doing real business (versus the "pretend" business of many dot.com companies), policy-makers made matters worse for large segments of the economy that, until then, were just barely able to make ends meet.

It's important to remember that most of the major companies that were associated with the tech bubble, such as Microsoft Corp. or Intel Corp., didn't need to borrow money then. Their major customers, however, had huge loans—probably taken out so they could buy new high-tech products. When Greenspan raised interest rates, they were hit hard as were hordes of people who had maxed out their lines of credit and personal loans. Realizing that the hike in rates was doing more harm than good, the government did a quick about-face and slashed interest rates. It was too late. Individuals and corporations alike had already slammed the brakes on their spending.

The impact of this crash was felt around the world. Faced with declining demand from one of the largest markets, and the ensuing collapse in consumer activity on the home front, governments rushed to prop up their economies by implementing expansionary monetary and fiscal policies. They were forced to reduce interest rates to encourage consumers to spend (just like the U.S. was doing), and increased government spending to create jobs.

Global Decline
Since the American dollar is the currency of global trade, then whatever the U.S. government does influences every single country in the world. As one economy after another began shrinking at an alarming rate while the U.S. economy geared down, governments initiated a massive concerted effort to stop the decline and kick-start their flailing economies.

Then, the unthinkable happened. The deadliest attack on the U.S. since Pearl Harbor occurred on September 11, 2001, when terrorists attacked the twin towers of the World Trade Center in New York. Its results were felt instantaneously around the world.

Everyone froze, waiting for the Americans to react and respond to this horrific assault. International efforts to repair the global economy were put on hold indefinitely, and then were further delayed by the subsequent invasions of Afghanistan and Iraq.

Despite the human and economic carnage caused by these world events, the Chinese and Indian economies continued to flourish, and they bought up most of the available global supply of raw materials. At the same time, other countries stopped buying resources at their usual rates because of the downturn in their economies. Faced with diminishing demands for their materials, mining companies and forestry firms slowed down or halted production.

Only when it looks like the global economy is going to recover will resource companies consider resuming or stepping up production. Until then, they're reluctant to do so, simply because it's an incredibly expensive mistake if the market isn't ready for their products or if buyers are unable to pay a reasonable price for the supplies. The resource companies would be saddled with exploration costs that will take years to recover, and stuck with expensive inventories, just after they've managed to survive almost twenty years in a depressed market. Taking the risk when the economy is still shaky is almost a recipe for bankruptcy.

Imminent Rebound

Governments in North America and Europe are doing their best to kick-start their economies but the time-honored steps of lowering interest rates and funding large projects—that have always put their economies back on track in the past—simply aren't working as fast as they used to.

Yet the positive signs that a rebound is imminent are starting to appear. The global demand for resources is beginning to improve, the Far East is growing again, and over the past year, commodity prices are heading in the right direction—as is to be expected at the start of global economic boom.

The prices of gold (gold bullion always seems to be the first to rise when good times are about to begin in the resources sector), nickel and copper have been creeping up, and other resources are expected to follow suit. It's only logical to expect rising demand and limited supply to cause prices to soar. This is especially true with commodity prices, as history can be our guide.

And once the "war premium"—the added value given to resources when any global power, such as the U.S. and Britain, is at war—is stripped from energy prices, then global prosperity will propel the prices of these natural resources even higher.

The economic scenario that is developing today is like a gigantic oil tanker loading just offshore. Once the engines are turning and the vessel is headed on a particular course, it takes a long time to stop or even alter the course of the tanker. The global economy is like that tanker—fueled up, running, and beginning to accelerate. It's hard to imagine anything that could slow it down once it gets going. Fueled by the demand for natural resources from emerging economies like India and China—and supplemented by growing demand for products from developed economies—there's not much likelihood of the momentum slowing down for many years to come.

Chapter Two
The Canadian Resource Sector

Canadians have always been known as "hewers of wood and drawers of water" in reference to two most plentiful natural resources in our country. It's no coincidence that the fur trappers who first explored this country established traditions that drive our economy even today. Visit any mining exploration camp and you'll find that the thrill of discovery is still the common denominator that drives modern-day pioneers toward success.

It would have been impossible to accomplish what the pioneers did if they hadn't combined an entrepreneurial flair with meticulous organizational skills. They established a network of trade centers, trails, canoe routes and outposts that ensured their explorations would be an economic success. Now railroads and highways, even air transportation in some cases, mean that today's explorers can efficiently and cost-effectively access the remote reservoirs of natural resources.

Canada's transportation infrastructure makes our country one of the world's most stable resource suppliers. The resource industry began with fur trading, but our system of government, transportation networks, telecommunications and export finance has ensured that gold and base-metal mining, forest product harvesting and paper manufacturing, and energy and petrochemical derivative industries are supported like no other place in the world.

International Hurdles

Drawing on their knowledge and expertise, Canadian companies have gone around the world to find new supplies of resources. Canada's Falconbridge Ltd., Inco Ltd., Aur Resources Inc., Barrick Gold Corp., Placer Dome Inc., Petro-Canada Ltd., Canadian Natural Resources Ltd. and many others are exploring and discovering raw materials around the globe, developing and delivering them to markets where they're in high demand.

Other countries try to clone the tax incentives that are available to Canadian corporations and people who invest in the natural resource industry, but seldom do they get the same successful results.

Many times Canadian resource companies have been seriously hurt because they assumed other governments and cultures play by the same rules. Both internationally experienced corporations and junior exploration start-ups have run into problems when they ventured into resource-rich but lesser-developed countries and the results have sometimes been devastating for investors. Rules governing ownership don't apply, don't exist, or simply aren't upheld by local authorities. Therefore, despite the potential for huge returns, the hurdles can be insurmountable. Canadian companies have sometimes lost everything they've invested in exploring for diamonds in Sierra Leone, gold in Russia, or oil in Kazakhstan. One case that was covered extensively in the Canadian media was Talisman Energy Inc. In March 2003, Talisman succumbed to public and investor pressure and completed the sale of its indirectly held interest in the Greater Nile project in Sudan.

Closer to Home

Another drawback or shortcoming is that although the infrastructure in Canada is efficient, it is expensive. When resources are discovered and mined on foreign soil, even the most enterprising domestic operation cannot compete with the lower costs of production of off-shore ventures. For example, Goldcorp Inc. is the lowest cost miner of gold in Canada, and the average cash cost per ounce was $100 in 2003. By comparison, the cash cost of an ounce of gold from Meridian Gold's El Peñón mine in Chile was $48 per ounce.

Price will be less and less of an issue in the near future. As the global economy picks up speed, the demand for both Canadian know-how and raw materials will be so strong that the higher cost of production will no longer be such a deterrent. Manufacturers will be willing to pay higher prices just to get the resources they need.

Consumer demand also fuels the resources market. Since the early 1980s, demand for resources has remained relatively stagnant. Low commodity prices meant that mining operations, for example, were no longer such profitable ventures, so owners shut them down.

The resulting consolidation of suppliers in the resource sector during the last twenty years was not motivated by greed, but survival. Low prices, diminished demand, declining inventories, high exploration and production costs have caused the resource sector to suffer for years. Things were made even worse because supply decreased at the same time as demand, so instead of spending money on improving or expanding their operations, resource companies were forced to become lean and mean.

Stronger than Ever
The good news is that the remaining companies are stronger than ever before, which puts them in an excellent position to meet the new demands from manufacturers at home and abroad. Unfortunately, one of their biggest hurdles won't necessarily be gearing up to supply the raw materials to meet the demand—it could very well be generating enough support from investors.

Resource companies continue to be haunted by the stigma of being risky ventures. Everyone knows of somebody who took a beating by investing in resource stocks, even though they could be the first person to suggest investing in gold when the market crashes. Of course, it's always somebody else who got battered by resources, as few people are keen to admit to their own failures in the investment world. Either that, or people just don't want to admit that they invested in this sector in the first place.

Many investors got burned in one of the biggest crashes in the resource sector when the oil and gas market imploded at the tail end of the energy boom in the early 1980s. At the time, oil and gas prices were as hot as the Calgary real estate market with no end in sight.

Everyone thought they would just keep rising, a premise that sparked one of the most embarrassing government initiatives in the last few decades: the National Energy Program (NEP)—the scheme by the feds in the late 1970s to buy a stake in the energy sector that eventually drove out most of the foreign investments. It failed miserably and decimated the once-strong sector for many years to come. Shortly after the NEP took effect, many CEOs of large multi-national energy companies flatly admitted they would no longer spend any more exploration or development dollars in Canada—simply because of the NEP.

Lessons Learned

Like all investment failures, lessons were learned from the crash of the oil and gas market. The first lesson reinforced the fact that resources are commodities, and commodity prices are always cyclical. So when investment analysts, economists and the media make strong cases for prices to rise indefinitely, then you can bet shares are about to plummet in value.

The second lesson dictated that whenever governments feel compelled to get involved in a resource sector, presumably to "protect national interests," then you can be sure they'll ruin the natural cyclical nature of the market. It's always nice when they eventually lose interest and allow market forces to rectify the situation.

Despite these painful lessons, investors shouldn't be intimidated by or avoid the sector. Doing so will mean you'll miss out on some of the most spectacular gains that can be had in the stock market. It seems ridiculous that the same investors who rode Nortel up to $120 in the summer months of 2000 and then down to 75 cents in October 2002, or traded Research In Motion up to $216 in March of 2000 and back down to $16 in October of 2002, will say that resource stocks are too volatile, too risky, too unknown.

In fact, resources have been a major part of investment portfolios for centuries. The first real investors in Canadian resources were the European royalty who bankrolled the early explorers. Sure they were keen to expand their empires, but they were also banking on trade in natural resources as a lucrative source of income.

Major Players

Today, resources continue to form the basis of growth and expansion in Canada through some of the country's largest publicly listed companies such as Inco Ltd., Falconbridge Ltd., Abitibi-Consolidated Inc. and Petro-Canada Ltd. (established in 1975 by Parliament, this is a crown corporation designed to create a strong Canadian presence in the oil industry). All are major global players and companies that every investor should track—although not necessarily always have in their portfolios.

It's also important for investors to monitor companies that initially appear to be borderline "promotes." Barrick Gold Corp. is a good example of this as it grew from a minor gold exploration company into one of the largest gold producers in the world, with mining interests in Argentina, Australia, Canada, Chile, Peru, Tanzania and the U.S.

Peter Munk, who is still chairman of Barrick Gold, founded the company back in 1983. He lucked out by unearthing the massive Goldstrike Deposit on the Carlin Trend in Nevada. Cynics didn't think it could be mined, but Munk was confident that there had to be an innovative means of extracting the gold efficiently and economically (the twin pillars of a profitable mining venture) even though the site was extremely challenging.

Munk and his team were the main factor behind the success of Barrick. This is a good example for investors as the qualifications and experience of the management team is a key indicator of the potential success of a company. A large part of investing in resource companies is learning to assess the people who run them.

Companies such as Barrick Gold ended up blazing the trail internationally for some of Canada's newer industries, such as telecommunications and technology. They tackle the challenges of doing business internationally: currency exchange hedging and translation issues, cultural obstacles, as well economic and political instability.

Although we live in an age when it is possible for money managers to specialize in one sector or another while working as a part of a team of other industry specialists, it wasn't always the case. Because resources are such a fundamental part of the Canadian investment landscape, portfolio managers who were trained as generalists have always had to track the resource sectors, and gradually branched out into monitoring telecommunications, financial services and technology as the need arose. Now they should be keeping a close eye on resources as it enters a sustainable longer-term cycle, one that will make the sector shine.

A Bad Rap

Are you still skeptical? Does Bre-X keep coming to mind? The truth is that if there's an opportunity to scam people into parting with their savings then it will be tried, and sometimes it will succeed. Bre-X received a great deal of attention in the press and dampened investor (both average and professional alike) enthusiasm for gold stocks. However since then, we've suffered through the demise of Enron Corp., which bilked investors and employees alike for millions. Coupled with a multitude of dot.com snakeoil salesmen who made off with millions, it makes mining-stock promoters look almost squeaky clean by comparison.

A simple rule of thumb is that if someone is trying to sell you something, then chances are it's a bad idea. If this is always the case, then you shouldn't be buying stocks at all, never mind resource stocks.

The quantity of scam artists is also directly proportional to how well a sector has performed. When the price of copper is climbing steadily, it's remarkable how many upstart companies with a prospective copper deposit will surface. Some are legitimate geologists and engineers who might have worked for a larger company and became frustrated by the lack of financial backing or corporate red tape. They decide to go out on their own to do what they love doing—exploring and discovering ore bodies. If these guys are out there when copper prices are lousy, not just when they're rocking and rolling, then in all likelihood they're not only legitimate, they're highly determined. These are important ingredients for success in any business initiative.

The willingness of investors to jump on the bandwagon is fodder for promoters. These guys typically have a smooth pitch, and are notably lacking geological or engineering credentials. All they hope to do is convince some unsuspecting bloke to turn his savings over to them.

Since the average investor tends only to consider resources in his portfolio when they're on a roll (which is too late as we've explained earlier), then it's statistically likely that the investor will succumb to the promoter's advances. Generally, if investors buy stocks when they are out-of-favor, then the odds of getting ripped off are much slimmer. If you want to invest, you have to do your homework. And if you've done your homework, the odds are good that you're making an intelligent move.

Like Other Sectors

Investing in resources is not all that much different from investing in any other sector. For producers, the upfront capital costs are much larger relative to some service industries, such as software. Yet if you compare it to industries like cable TV, telecommunications equipment or auto parts manufacturing, the capital commitment isn't over the top. These are all mature industries; therefore, they are always going to be cyclical.

When the economy is tanking, businesses and consumers spend less so sales for goods such as computer hardware predictably plummet, with the rare exception of some anomalous blips. For example, the threat of the Y2K millennium bug caused a short but secular (as opposed to cyclical) growth binge for computer software and hardware. The panic to avoid having systems crash when the clock hit the year 2000 created a large demand—even if most of the demand was artificial—for computer software and subsequent hardware upgrades as well. Many mistook the increased demand as a boom for the bits-and-bytes industry, but these false hopes were thoroughly squashed when the tech bubble finally burst in the spring of 2000.

In many respects, understanding resources is less difficult than understanding the high-tech or telecommunications industries. The key starting point is getting a grip on where the resources stand in relation to other sectors. Before other industries begin the first leg of a new business cycle, they'll demand more raw materials. This is why it is so important to do your research before the cycle gets going.

Many economics textbooks try to explain or rationalize why there are business cycles. Forget them. It's infinitely easier to just accept that cycles happen. This chapter has explained why a new business cycle in Canadian resources has just begun. Now subsequent chapters will help you understand which natural resources will be the first to benefit from accelerating economic activity and when. Educating yourself means it's not too late to cash in on the coming global economic boom in resources.

People are generally lazy, and investors are only human after all. So when there's an abundance of press, research reports and everyday experience, people are lulled into believing they actually know more about technology, banking and other basic industries than they do. Unless the resource sector is trending towards a cyclical peak, there's little publicity except bad publicity. Having read the book so far, then you know that this is the best time to act.

The most important point to remember is that resources are the first sector to feel the brunt of looming recessions and depressions. When businesses further down the chain start experiencing softer demand for their products and services, and their products come under pricing pressure, they are quick to ask their suppliers (including resource companies) to ship less and charge less. Watch for these signs because when they start to appear, it's time to say goodbye to your resource stocks.

In the meantime, enjoy the boom.

CHAPTER THREE
Diamonds

Diamonds are called many things by the people who covet them. Marilyn Monroe crooned "Diamonds are a Girl's Best Friend." Today's hip-hop and rap artists simply refer to them as "bling bling" for their ability to dazzle and impress.

Diamonds have always been valuable, purely for emotional reasons. Since ancient times, people have trolled the rocky banks of rivers, keeping their eyes peeled for the sparkling stones that could be cut, polished and worn with pride—or sold for a king's ransom.

These days, people are just as intent on finding diamonds and making their fortune. It's well worth their time—if they strike it lucky, that is. It takes almost as much time, effort and money to discover metals or gemstones but the rewards vary greatly. In 2003, a pound of copper sold for over $75, while a pound of gold was worth about $4,500. According to Bob Gannicott, president and CEO of Aber Diamond Corp., Canada's second diamond producing mine, a pound of their rough run-of-mine diamonds (pre-cut and pre-polished) are worth about US$172,800.

Diamond in the Rough
Although the price of diamonds fluctuates based on product quality and several other factors, the average price of rough diamonds has

remained relatively steady for years. In 2003, prices started to climb, which was good news for the fledgling Canadian diamond mining companies.

The value of rough diamonds increases approximately ten times: $5 billion of rough diamonds from a supplier would fetch over $56 billion after they've been cut, polished and set in jewelry for sale at retail prices.

Rough diamonds are literally dug out of the ground, whereas a polished diamond is ready to be set in a ring. As a result, there's quite a size difference between the two. For example, the world's largest rough diamond was over three thousand carats, while the world's largest polished diamond was five hundred and twenty carats. To put it all into perspective, a good size diamond ring is around one carat...imagine a rock over five hundred times that size.

If you cut away the emotional value, then a diamond is really just a freak of nature. It's simply carbon (the exact same stuff as the graphite lead in pencils) that is compressed by molten rock then pushed to the surface of the earth in volcanic pipes made of kimberlite. Not all kimberlite pipes have diamonds in them, so they're classified as either diamondiferous (diamond-bearing and sometimes lucrative) or non-diamondiferous (absolutely worthless). The combination of heat, pressure and the push to the surface of the earth changes the chunks of carbon into the most brilliant, valuable and hardest substance known to man.

Making the Grade
The primary use of diamonds is to cut, polish and then set them in jewelry. The market is hotter than ever for rings, earrings and necklaces featuring the sparkling stones: in the last fifteen years, the jewelry market for diamonds has grown by over 250%. Scrap or inferior diamonds are used in commercial applications. Set on the cutting edges of drills and other tools, the diamond-edge means they can literally cut through anything.

A stone is valued on the basis of the four "Cs":
  • Carat (The size of the stone. One carat weighs 1/5 of a gram.)
  • Clarity (Some are graded as flawless but most are ranked on a

complex system of letters and numbers, which classifies how clear or transparent the stone is.)

• Cut (You name it, they're doing it. No longer just round, pear, brilliant or emerald shapes. Lasers are working wonders with these impervious gems, carving and cutting them into shapes that were until recently impossible to do.)

• Color (White or colorless gems are the most valuable. Diamonds are also brown, green, pink, orange, blue, black, yellow and—the rarest of all—red. Canadian diamonds tend to have "high color" as they're very white. This is the color that is most valued by Americans, the world's largest diamond consumers.)

Why is this important information for investors? Because you need to know what type and quality of diamonds the company has unearthed in order to gauge the probability of them being the next De Beers (the world's largest diamond company), or if they'll fade into obscurity and leave you empty-handed.

Canadian Diamond Mines
Although exploration for diamonds started in the Canadian north in the early 1970s, the big rush didn't occur until 1991 when Dia Met Minerals Ltd. and BHP Billiton Diamonds Inc. discovered diamond-bearing kimberlite pipes at Point Lake in the Northwest Territories. Chuck Fipke and Stewart Blusson are the now-famous geologists who discovered what eventually became the Ekati Mine. Fipke is the epitome of the true Canadian pioneer, spending most of his life wandering around the wilderness breaking rocks, driven by an unfettered determination to find diamonds.

The Point Lake discovery sparked the largest staking rush in Canadian history as explorers laid claim to more than fifty million acres. "Over three hundred and fifty companies held land positions," recalls Randy Turner, president and CEO of Diamondex Resources Ltd. in Vancouver, and a veteran Canadian diamond explorer. "At the end of the rush, only eight were left."

The next big discovery was in 1994 when Aber Resources Ltd. (now Aber Diamond Corp.) of Toronto and Kennecott Canada Exploration discovered the Diavik deposits. Then Winspear Resources Ltd. and Aber unearthed the Snap Lake reserves in 1996.

Four years later, they sold the site to De Beers for $480 million in what was the first diamond-mining takeover in Canadian history.

The sector really took off when Canada's first diamond mine, the Ekati Mine, opened in 1998. The mine is estimated to have a twenty-year lifespan, and is expected to produce almost five million carats each year, with an average value of over $130 per carat.

Next to start production was the Diavik Mine, which opened in early 2003. Like Ekati, it has an estimated lifespan of twenty years, but its production is expected to be somewhat higher than the Ekati Mine. It's slated to produce over six million carats annually, with an average value of over $78 per carat.

The Snap Lake Mine is expected to commence operations in 2006 (full production in 2007). Like the other two Canadian mines, it is expected to last for roughly twenty years, but it will likely produce less than half of what each of the other two mines put out annually, at an estimated $100 per carat.

The price per carat is an indicator of the quality (the clarity, color and size) of the diamonds found in each mine.

Diamonds have also been discovered in Nunavut and in Quebec, while the world's largest kimberlites (volumetrically) have been unearthed in Saskatchewan.

An Investment Opportunity
Even with this impressive track record, many people are still not convinced that there are diamonds in Canada. Eventually the news will sink in as Canada becomes the world's third largest producer of these valuable chunks of carbon (behind Botswana and Russia) and will soon account for 15% of the world's diamond supplies.

The lack of knowledge of most Canadians, let alone American or overseas investors, about the burgeoning diamond industry represents a tremendous investment opportunity for people to buy shares in Canadian diamond mining companies now. Once the rest of the world realizes that there really are diamonds in Canada then the shares will be in big demand by international investors.

What does that mean for you? Well, if you're lucky enough to include in your portfolio one explorer that discovers a potentially economic diamond deposit, then you'll do very well. In fact, out of a

modest list of no more than ten different stocks, all you need is one
to be a big winner, and that will more than make up for the ones that
flop. This is why professional investors always use a shotgun rather
than a rifle-shot approach when it comes to investing in diamond
companies.

Government Support
It's been a great relief to mining entrepreneurs and their investors
that the provincial and federal governments have been extremely
helpful with regards to the development of diamond mines.
Canada has a legacy of exploration, which makes it unique in the
sense that governments tend to encourage resource exploration and
development.

This historical legacy has created a diamond-mining climate that
is stable and environmentally friendly. Nunavut, Canada's youngest
province, even appointed a Minister of Sustainable Development to
demonstrate their commitment to the resource sector.

Inevitably the prospect of riches will tempt politicians. The
western premiers initiated a national diamond strategy at their July
2003 conference and the premier of the Northwest Territories,
Stephen Kakfwi, stated, "We need to increase our participation in
this multi-billion dollar sector." In any other country, this would be
an ominous sign for investors. However, the western provinces are
experienced at nurturing resource industries; just take a look at
Alberta and what it has done to ease the way for the oil and gas
industry.

The only risk, which seems extremely remote at this early stage
in the diamond industry, is if something akin to the National Energy
Program (NEP) is introduced. The good news is that the NEP experience was a major catastrophe and Canadians have a long memory
when it comes to disastrous government intervention.

So far, the government's involvement has been good for the fledgling diamond industry, and the foreseeable future looks even better.
Remote communities are looking forward to having challenging,
rewarding and local jobs for their children. New schools, government
services and ancillary businesses of every variety are emerging, and
will continue to do so as the mines develop and prosper. It makes

sense for the government to support this industry as economic growth means more prosperous taxpayers.

Blood-free diamonds
The only downside of Canadian diamond mining is that a highly skilled workforce must toil in a hostile natural environment far away from civilization. That means the cost of extracting diamonds is quite high. Definitely much higher than the world's leading producers where miners are paid a fraction of what Canadian teams take home.

While it costs more to retrieve the stones and deliver them to market, Canadian diamonds are being sold at a premium price because they're "blood-free" and top quality. As a result, they command higher prices in the global marketplace than diamonds from Russia or Botswana.

"Blood-free" diamonds is a term that refers to the fact that the miners are not slaves nor is the money from the sale of the diamonds being used to finance military regimes or ruthless cartels. The problem is that you can't tell the difference between a bloody diamond and a "blood-free" diamond. Only certificates and stamps separate the two.

Consultants advise retailers to avoid using the term "blood-free" to describe their diamond jewelry as it is a negative term that could reflect badly on the entire industry. It's clear that diamonds from Canada have other attributes that are guaranteed to make them more desirable than those from other top-producing nations. A stable government and the professionalism of the companies in the sector ensure that polishers and retailers will be able to count on a steady supply of top-quality diamonds. They know that the supply of Canadian diamonds will not be stopped by civil war or political strife.

And what a supply it will be. Diamonds in the Ekati Mine are estimated to be worth well over $10 billion. The Diavik Mine is valued at more than $9.5 billion. The next diamond deposit slated to go into production is Snap Lake, with a deposit worth about $7.8 billion. These three mines have added approximately $30 billion to Canada's mineral net worth.

Investing in Diamond Mines

Is it too late to invest in diamond exploration since all of these major discoveries have already been made? Hardly. In fact, the timing is just perfect as the industry is still in its infancy. Dozens of junior and a few intermediate exploration companies are busy searching for the next big diamond deposit.

Some of the juniors worth keeping an eye on include:

• Diamondex Resources Ltd. is a Vancouver-based diamond exploration and development company. It was created in 1999 as a spinoff of Winspear Diamonds Ltd. after Winspear was sold to De Beers. It owns the right to explore for diamonds on more than seven and a half million acres.

• Ashton Mining of Canada Inc. is a diamond exploration company headquartered in North Vancouver, B.C. Since its launch in 1993, it has bought rights to properties in Alberta, Nunavut, the Northwest Territories and Quebec.

• Diamonds North Resources Ltd. In 2002, Major General Resources divided into two different companies: Commander Resources, concentrating on gold, nickel and base metals, and Vancouver's Diamonds North Resources, which focused exclusively on diamond exploration in Canada's far north.

• Stornoway Diamond Corp. of Vancouver has five project areas in Nunavut, the Northwest Territories and Quebec. Second only to De Beers with regards to its total land holdings in Canada, Stornoway's teams are exploring for diamonds in more than eleven million acres.

• Tahera Corp. is a Canadian diamond exploration and development company with headquarters in Toronto. It began staking claims and exploring in 1992 and acquired a large land position; today it has properties in Nunavut and the Northwest Territories and in and around the Slave Craton, a region which so far has been home to most of Canada's major diamond discoveries.

• Majescor Resources is taking a chance on exploring for diamonds in northern Quebec and given Ashton's luck, they could be on the right track.

Signs of Growth

Luxury goods are a unique market, and an excellent example of what economists call an "inelastic" demand curve. If the price is increased, people want them; if the price is decreased, people still want them. What's fascinating about the diamond industry is that it's a virtual oligopoly as a handful of companies work closely together to control supply and prices. This almost guarantees that the industry will always be profitable and that the cost of diamond jewelry will either be stable or increase. All indicators point to their continued success.

Two key factors are also worth keeping in mind:

• Since the terrorist attack on the World Trade Center in New York on September 11, 2001, diamonds have outperformed any other luxury good. In the last quarter of 2001, there were more diamond retail sales than during any other quarter.

• The fastest growing economies in the world today (China and India) are demanding more luxury goods.

"Our latest forecasts show demand for diamonds continuing to rise during our long-term forecast period until 2012, based on current and projected GDP forecasts in all the key markets," says Charles Wyndham, co-founder of WWW International Diamond Consultants Ltd. in the U.K.

However, there are a few trends that give players in the diamond retail industry some gray hairs. One major concern is that as prices of diamonds rise, the public could pressure retailers to reduce the diamond size, quality or content in order to keep a lid on the cost of buying jewelry.

The other large concern is the possible impact of synthetics. Most experts dismiss this concern arguing that as long as the average purchaser can distinguish between synthetics and diamonds, then the diamond market is OK.

The Canadian Advantage

Why should you choose Canadian diamond mining companies if you're interested in investing in this volatile sector? There are many reasons, namely:

• Cut and color may become more important than the current top standard of quality. Canadian diamonds are white, clear and a good size so they rate high on this evaluation. The high prices commanded by these diamonds offsets the higher costs of production in Canada.

• Less investor risk. Canada is the world's most stable major diamond producer. There are no wars, no Russian mafia, no political instability, and exploration companies don't have to worry that the government will appropriate their claims once they discover the diamonds.

• Potential for branding Canadian diamonds, like the popular Polar Bear diamonds by Sirius Diamonds Ltd. of Vancouver. The key benefit of this is that it clearly marks them as "blood-free" diamonds. As more people become ethical consumers, this will increase the demand.

• Other diamond-producing countries are decreasing production as mines have been mined out and/or they're just not finding new ones. No new discoveries in Russia, and nothing in Australia since the Argyle Mine in the 1980s.

• Canadian mines have to follow strict environmental regulations and high safety standards, a factor that not only makes them better employers, but also should appeal to the growing number of ethical mutual funds.

The Risks, The Rewards
Diamonds are so incredibly valuable that dozens of companies are willing to invest millions of dollars in searching for them. If they unearth the gems, they'll reap an incredible return on their investment. The risks are tremendous, simply because it's extremely difficult to find kimberlite in the first place, and even more uncommon to locate diamondiferous kimberlite. But the payoff is worth it.

A few lucky companies will make more money than their directors ever dreamed possible. Diamond mines can have a long life—some up to fifty years—and can produce over $50 billion in rough diamonds during their lifespan. The Canadian mines to date have a shorter expected lifespan, with relatively lower levels of production.

The odds, as mentioned earlier, are not in favor of the explorers. First, they have to discover a region with kimberlites. Then the work really begins. So far, over six thousand kimberlites have been discovered globally, but only forty-eight became producing diamond mines. More than 86% weren't diamondiferous at all, and of the small percentage that were, only a fraction hosted enough sizable diamonds to make it worthwhile to build a mine. The risk—and the cost—is that the companies spend millions of dollars on exploration and research long before they know that their search is all for naught.

The Diavik Mine, for example, cost over $1.3 billion to build, while the Ekati Mine had an initial cost of $1 billion. They were both massive and expensive undertakings. It's testimony to the lucrative nature of the diamond mining industry that despite the astronomical costs, the profits still make it all worthwhile. The Ekati Mine paid for itself in just two years of production.

A "Sure Thing"
Investing in intermediate Canadian diamond companies is an opportunity to invest in one of the few "sure things" in the resource sector. BHP Billiton (Ekati Mine and others) and Aber Diamond Corp. (Diavik Mine) are publicly traded companies with relatively little risk of disappointing—the diamonds are there, it's just a matter of time before they're dug out. Once they are, a burgeoning market will pay top dollar for these blood-free, high-quality diamonds.

More adventurous investors will choose to invest in exploration companies. Several have real prospects, like Ashton Mining, who has discovered a piece of diamond-filled tundra on their property. The catch is that it's going to be some time before they'll know if there are enough large diamonds in the deposit to justify building a mine.

Some of the junior companies—ones that are just at the exploration stage and haven't produced any diamonds—are managed by extremely capable and accomplished teams who are determined to locate the next great Canadian diamond deposit.

Because of the unique pricing structure in the diamond industry, it's not really important whether the global demand for diamonds is going to increase or not. What is important is that the marketing companies and jewelry producers need a steady supply of top-quality diamonds to meet the demand of the market that they essentially control.

If the junior exploration companies discover diamonds, then the producers will want to buy the gems. This is the main reason why geologists keep slogging away in the frozen tundra—all they have to do is find the diamonds to ensure the reward. It's in sharp contrast to the gold or other resources markets. Even if a mine is producing the best quality gold in the world, if the price on the open market drops, the owners could lose a fortune. Many gold mining companies closed down their operations in the past because their production costs ended up being higher than the price they could get for selling the gold in the market.

Since the pricing in the diamond market works differently, it makes it easier for stock promoters to get in on the game. With such an eager and lucrative market waiting for the next great diamond discovery, it's relatively easy for someone with nothing more than a few acres of moose pasture in the Yukon to convince naive investors into buying their stock. That's why it's so important to do some research and manage your expectations before making an investment.

Researching the Prospects
It's not difficult these days to get information about prospective investments, thanks to the Internet. Most companies have excellent Web sites, that contain a lot of details essential to the investor.

Start by scanning the backgrounds of the management team and the company directors. Are they geologists? How long have they been in the industry? What projects have they worked on? You'll find that Canadian diamond mining is a pretty small club and a few names keep popping up, especially pioneers like Chuck Fipke, Stewart Blusson, Randy Turner and Eira and her father Grenville Thomas, most of whom have gone on to head up some of the most promising companies after paying their dues digging away in the north. They've all logged their hours and the only thing that separates one from the other is luck. Like the joke says: "Hire a lucky geologist, not necessarily a good one."

Click on the media section of the Web sites and read the press releases to learn how far along the company is in terms of its exploration programs.

Some companies are still following indicator minerals, hoping to find a kimberlite source. (Kimberlite is made up of unique types of minerals. If a geologist finds traces of these types of minerals, called "indicator minerals," in the samples then the odds are increased that diamond-bearing pipes of kimberlite could be found in the site.) As mentioned earlier in the chapter, this means they've still got a long way to go before they'll find diamonds...or come up empty-handed.

Other companies are more advanced, having already collected bulk samples that contain diamonds, but it's still too early to tell whether the diamonds are large enough or if there are enough of them to constitute an "economic" deposit. Rough diamonds have to be large enough in individual size to fetch enough money from the polishers; and there has to be enough of these large gems to cover the incredibly high cost of getting them out of the earth.

Once you've done the first round of reading about diamond companies, turn to your advisor for information. Keep in mind that because this part of the investment game is classified as being highly speculative or risky, advisors will usually want some assurance that you can and will tolerate the risk. No matter how talented and experienced an exploration team might be, if they fail to find diamonds, you end up with squat.

And it could take a long time before the diamonds are brought to market, a major hurdle for the sector and the primary reason behind investor fatigue. Putting it bluntly, if you can't take the stress and tension waiting for a discovery—or tolerate the loss if there isn't one—then you'd be wise to invest your money elsewhere.

Chapter Four
Gold

"You keep me searching for a heart of gold," warbled Neil Young, a real Canadian resource in his own right. More than thirty years after this song hit the charts, investors are well-positioned to find their own heart of gold.

Gold has always been one of the leading commodities in the resource sector despite its ups and downs in the market over the past twenty years. It lost most of its brilliance when it hit a low of just over US$250 per ounce in 1999. Now a declining production outlook and rising demand combined with record-low interest rates are driving up the price of this precious metal.

Some analysts are expecting gold to head back up to 1983 rates when it topped US$500 per ounce. Others suggest it could go as high as US$800 per ounce within the decade. At any rate, investors are once again taking a shine to this gleaming resource.

GOLD PRICE OVER 10 YEARS (fig. 2)

Gold Rush

Gold is considered to be one of the first metals discovered and used extensively by man, primarily for decorative purposes. Just think of all of those pictures of the Egyptian pharaohs, draped from head to toe in gold jewelry. Dreaming of riches, European royalty financed countless voyages by explorers in search of gold in the New World. Given its unique color and purity, gold has kept people spellbound for centuries.

Because it is beautiful, rare—and therefore valuable—its discovery usually sparked gold rushes where hordes of prospectors would swarm to an area where some poor sod had stumbled on a sparkling nugget. Word would spread quickly about his good fortune, and within months, he'd find himself surrounded by panhandlers and diggers staking their claims on the edge of his land in hopes of discovering their share of the elusive metal.

The major international gold rushes all occurred within the last one hundred and fifty years, starting with Australia in the mid 1800s. The South African gold rush was in Johannesburg in 1886, while Canada's began in 1897 in the Yukon. The largest U.S. gold strike was in the early 1900s in Nevada—home today for some of the world's largest gold companies. Regardless of where or when they staked their claim, prospectors only had one thing on their mind: to strike it rich by finding gold and selling or trading their booty to the highest bidder.

Back then gold was money—it only had to be weighed before it could be used as legal tender. This practice coined the term "the gold standard" which was a monetary standard primarily used from 1870 to 1914. Currencies were defined in terms of their gold content and were exchangeable for gold. Most nations adhered to the gold standard during the early 1900s, but gradually backed out of it over the years. Britain jumped ship in 1931 and the last time that a nation's currency was minted in gold was in 1933. When the U.S. dropped the gold standard in 1971, it was the last official link between gold and money in circulation.

Fluctuating Prices

Even though the gold standard is no longer in effect, gold is still widely considered to be the backbone of a financial system. Like currency, the price of gold continually rises and falls but not one economist, research analyst, investor or speculator can pinpoint the real reasons why bullion goes up and down.

What they do know for sure is that it has been climbing relatively steadily from a low of US$250 in 1999, regaining its luster in 2003, and at press time, had passed US$400 per ounce.

WORLDWIDE GOLD PRODUCTION AND INFLATED GOLD PRICE (fig. 3)

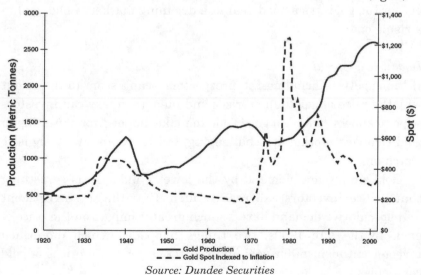

Source: Dundee Securities

The other sure thing is that as the price of gold rises, so does the level of interest of explorers. Like the early prospectors, they've got dollar signs in their eyes. The only real difference between the two is that these days most of them have geology or engineering degrees.

Exploration teams are driven by profit. If gold is selling for $250 per ounce, then it's not all that worthwhile for them to dig it up or even invest a lot of time and money on exploration. If gold is going for $500 per ounce, then the potential for significant profits after they get it out of the ground is more than enough incentive for companies to keep on exploring.

Although gold is more precious on a per ounce basis than base metals such as copper, nickel or zinc, the challenge is that the price of gold bullion is also extremely sensitive to market conditions.

Gold is actively traded in the spot and futures markets. Also known as a cash market, a "spot market" is where commodities such as gold are bought and sold for cash and delivered immediately. A "futures market" is where contracts for the future delivery of a commodity are bought and sold. In the last few decades, this trading has enabled gold producers to routinely hedge their future gold production. Selling gold that they haven't got out of the ground (which is known as "hedging") guarantees the price they'll get for the gold. It's a good deal in a declining market; a bad deal in a rising one.

Downward Spiral

If the experts—including the prospectors—can't seem to figure out why the price of gold bullion rises and falls, then how can investors hope to know when it's a good time to make money from investing in gold company stocks? It's challenging, but there are many signs to watch for.

Gold supply and demand by the jewelry industry is something that novice investors can readily identify with, but investment and speculative demand have a much greater impact on the price of gold. In the late 1990s, two things happened which dampened investor enthusiasm for gold and shattered the share prices of gold companies.

The first major event was the technology bubble (or more precisely, the mania to own high-tech and telecommunications stocks) and then the subsequent spike in interest rates. In an effort to diminish what U.S. Federal Reserve Chairman Alan Greenspan called "irrational exuberance" towards high-tech stocks, he hiked interest rates in the U.S. Rates around the world rose in tandem, since the U.S. dollar is the de facto currency of global trade and commerce. The problem for the gold industry was that as interest rates rose, the opportunity cost of holding on to a non-interest bearing asset such as gold became too high.

The double whammy hit the market hard. Aggressive investors dumped their gold and gobbled up high-tech stocks. Conservative investors avoided both markets, and clung to their bonds and T-bills. The price of gold plummeted.

Enter the speculators. When the price of gold is declining, commodity traders are inclined to sell short, meaning they'll "borrow" a specific amount of gold and sell it on the open market. Later, they'll purchase the same amount of gold (hopefully at a lower price) to "pay back" the loan. They get to pocket the difference. The catch is that the downward spiral of the price of gold then becomes self-propelled.

Making it worse were the bumbling moves made by central banks around the world that buy gold bullion for investment purposes—a throwback to the days when currencies were actually backed by gold reserves. Not necessarily known for their investment acumen, central banks contributed to the success of short-sellers by getting caught up in the panic and dumping their gold. The price of this precious metal was in free fall.

LONG/SHORT POSITIONS VERSUS GOLD PRICE (fig. 4)

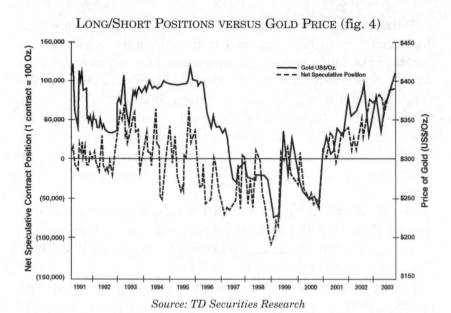

Source: TD Securities Research

As the chart above shows, things have changed dramatically. The U.S. Federal Reserve Board reversed its stance on interest rates so they dropped to a forty-year low in the last few years. The World Trade Center attack, retaliation in Afghanistan, and the subsequent war in Iraq put a lid on economic activity to the point where drastic remedial action by the government was required.

Declining interest rates—initiated with gusto by the feds—lowered the opportunity cost of buying gold. Since nobody wanted anything to do with high-tech or telecommunications stocks, and investors were fearful of another market bubble, people started looking at investing in gold once again. Historically, global unrest makes investors take a shine to this precious metal; perhaps due to the perceived security of gold as a traditional investment. As a result, investor demand for gold has been rising steadily in the past year.

Mining for Gold

The reason gold is valuable is because it's difficult to find deposits that are large enough to justify building a mine. And even when a sizable deposit is found, it can take years to get any gold out of it. Because of the low prices in the past decade, companies have not been investing in exploration. No exploration means no new supplies of gold are slated to be brought into production, and therefore existing gold mines are the only source of gold.

At first glance, it seems logical that investing in a gold mining company would be just like investing in a diamond mining company— after all, it's a luxury good and valuable because it is relatively rare. The key issue before investing in either diamond or gold stocks is to look beneath the surface to discover the real gems.

The main difference between gold and diamond mining is that the odds are much better that gold explorers will find a viable deposit. Gold, like diamonds, is a by-product of prehistoric volcanic activity, but there are far more gold deposits than there are diamondiferous ones.

Like diamond mining, gold mining in the past would begin when a nugget was found on the ground. These days, it's unusual to encounter any visible gold. As a result, mining techniques have had to become more sophisticated. Airborne magnetic surveys and satellite imagery help geologists identify prospective exploration targets long before any digging is done.

Once a prospective site is identified, samples of the rocks are analyzed in the laboratory. Because of technology, gold doesn't need to be found in large chunks anymore. As long as there's a consistent quantity of gold over a specific area—even if it's not much per ton— then mining engineers can still economically separate the precious metal from the surrounding rock.

Goldcorp Challenge

Discovering gold, or mining it, isn't as easy as it sounds. That's where ingenuity and creativity separates one company from another. One of the best examples of thinking outside of the box was when Toronto-based Goldcorp Inc. was determined to discover more gold in Red Lake, Ontario: the largest and one of the lowest-cost gold mines in Canada.

For the first time ever in the history of the secretive global gold mining industry, Rob McEwen, Goldcorp's chairman and CEO, threw caution to the wind and shared all of the information that Goldcorp had on its Red Lake claim in Ontario by posting it on the

Internet. A total prize of US$575,000 with a top award of US$95,000 were offered to the geologist or exploration company who could tell Goldcorp where they would find the next six million ounces of gold.

Hundreds of geologists from around the world were intrigued by the contest called the 2001 Goldcorp Challenge. Two Australian companies that produced a 3D model of the mine won the grand prize. Their proposal enabled Goldcorp to mine gold in a camp that everyone else had long written off as being spent.

Another example of the innovation by Canadian companies was in 1983 when Barrick Gold Corp. (formerly American Barrick) bought the massive Goldstrike Property in Nevada. Coming up with an efficient and cost-effective process to extract the metal was challenging. The most skeptical of all were the previous owners of the property who sold it to Peter Munk for a relative pittance. Through sheer determination, Munk and his team built the foundation for what today is a world-class gold producing company.

Supply and Demand

Now that the price of gold has started to rise, companies are spending more money on exploration. The problem is that even if they are unusually lucky and quickly discover new deposits, it will still take years before any gold will be produced. That means the only supply is from existing deposits and mines, a finite supply that is declining in quantity.

That's great news for investors as all the major factors—a rising stock market, record-low interest rates and a low supply of gold— mean that buying shares in gold exploration and production companies makes sense once again.

One factor that's not usually an important player in driving up the price of gold is the demand by manufacturers. Gold is valuable for two reasons: its scarcity and beauty. Soft and relatively easy to work with, it can be molded into jewelry or hammered into thin leaves which can be wrapped around virtually any object.

What most people don't know is that gold is also highly resistant to rust, corrosion and heat, so it is used in a variety of commercial applications. It can be found in a huge range of everyday products—

from CDs to dental fillings to electronics—as well as in sophisticated high-tech or aerospace applications. For example, thin layers of gold coat the cockpit windows of jets to protect pilots from the harmful effects of the sun's rays.

The only time that the supply of gold becomes a factor in the market price is when there's a shortage.

These are the reasons why leading gold producers have been unwinding their hedge positions. They brag that their companies are unhedged, arguing that it puts them in a stronger financial position. In fact, they're no longer hedging their product simply because it doesn't make sense in a strong market.

Hedging is a protective manoeuvre for producers. If prices are falling or have already hit bottom, then a company has nothing to lose by gambling that prices might start to rise at some point. Therefore, they sell some of their future gold production through a commodities exchange or bullion bank, which means buyers will pay them a pre-arranged (and higher than current market) price at a later date. But if the market for gold is strong and getting stronger every day, then companies aren't interested in selling future gold production at a pre-arranged fixed price. The odds are good that they will be able to get an even higher price than the pre-arranged one at a later date.

The risk of hedging is if a mine's production is forecasted to decline and little or no exploration is being done. A company will then be hard pressed to guarantee that they'll have any gold to sell in the future.

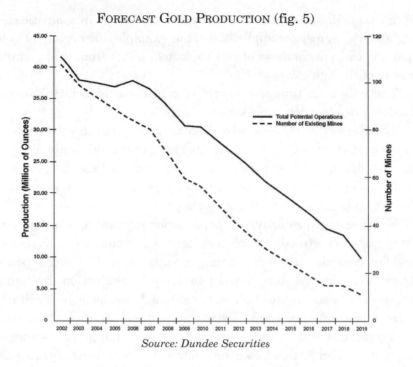

FORECAST GOLD PRODUCTION (fig. 5)

Source: Dundee Securities

Lower Risk, Lower Reward

Given all of the risks involved in gold mining, should investors concentrate on junior and intermediate exploration companies or just buy shares in senior gold producers? A junior company is one that hasn't discovered any gold yet, but is actively looking. An intermediate or mid-tier company is one that is producing gold (like a senior) but spending all of their revenues on exploration (like a junior). Senior companies are known entities with established assets, earnings records and credit ratings.

Conservative investors can take comfort in the fact that Barrick Gold and Placer Dome Inc. in Canada, and Anglo Gold and Newmont Mining Corp. (the world's largest gold producer) are at least producing gold. Larger companies also have the financial and technical experience to mine gold on a scale large enough to meet current demands.

As a result, the seniors are relatively more secure investments. The downside of this stability is that any returns they provide will likely be at a lower percentage gain than those from an investment in a successful junior or an intermediate company.

Generally, but not always, the lower the investment risk, the lower the potential reward is. That's why professional investors tend to devote time and energy to researching junior exploration companies and intermediate producers.

The larger global producers will still provide decent returns in a market boom, but they need large incremental increases to their gold reserves if they are to grow their business significantly. Big companies aren't particularly interested in spending their time and money exploring for gold deposits that in all likelihood will be too small to have a meaningful impact in their overall reserves and production. Management is more content to sit on the sidelines, buying shares in junior or intermediate companies. When the explorers find the proverbial motherlode, then the seniors can buy the entire company.

The same "big fish eat small fish" pattern occurs in other natural resource industries like energy. Creative geologists and determined engineers become frustrated by the seemingly excessive red tape in large corporations. They bemoan the curtailing of their work as exploration budgets get slashed when gold prices are in a slump. Frequently, these highly skilled professionals walk away from the stability and security of their large employers to become entrepreneurs, knowing full well that if they discover one of those motherlodes then their former employers will step up and pay a premium to buy their fledgling company. If their former employers aren't keen, then another large company that's in desperate need of gold will certainly buy them.

Luck and Hard Work

By doing a bit of homework, investors who include a selection of junior and intermediate gold companies in their portfolios can also profit handsomely from this same formula. The challenge is choosing which junior company will be the lucky one. As with diamond mining, sometimes the only factor that separates the successful players from the others is a bit of luck, being in the right place at the right time.

Take Northgate Exploration Ltd., for example. Terry Lyons, chairman, and Ken Stowe, president and CEO, pulled together an extremely capable team that has rehabilitated the Kemess Mines in northern B.C. Built for a cost of over $600 million by Royal Oak

Mines Ltd. (headed by CEO Peggy Witte), the mine went into production in 1998. One year later, Royal Oak appointed an interim
receiver. Northgate acquired the mine for roughly $280 million in
February 2000, and worked hard to grow the reserve base through a
methodical and successful exploration program.

Now it's full steam ahead for Kemess, thanks also to the fact that
the current provincial government is more hospitable towards
natural resource industries than was the case a decade ago. The
mine is producing record amounts of gold/copper concentrate just as
the markets for the metals are improving.

Another good example is Cumberland Resources. Kerry Curtis,
president and CEO, has a top-notch exploration and mine development team turning the Meadowbank gold deposit in Nunavut into
an even larger operation.

As in the case of diamond exploration, Canada's far north is ripe
for precious and base-metal exploration. In more populated parts of
the world there are many social and environmental hurdles that can
hinder resource exploration and production. In Canada's remote
northern communities, the jobs that are created are welcome, and
the environmentally responsible practices are some of the most
stringent in the world.

Go Big or Go Home
Like the major gold producers, many junior and intermediate gold
companies appreciate the economics of exploring and producing gold
in foreign countries. In South America, Africa and Asia, there are
gold deposits that can be extremely low cost to extract. The exploration teams know that there's gold in the ground because locals
have been mining it close to the surface for centuries. By applying
modern exploration, drilling and engineering techniques, the size of
the deposit can be pinpointed accurately and gold produced at a
fraction of the cost of extracting gold in Canada.

Because of the higher potential profits, the economics of overseas
mining is tempting but as many companies have found, it can be
fraught with a host of socio-political risks. Meridian Gold Inc. of
Nevada is an experienced intermediate producer with perhaps the
best growth prospects for a company its size. They own an extremely

promising reserve in Esquel, Argentina, but they encountered tremendous local resistance to their plans for developing the mine. When the news broke in North America about their local difficulties, the stock price took a beating.

There are many foreign projects underway by Canadian companies, such as Bema Gold Corp. in Russia; Southwestern Resources Corp. in China and other countries; Bolivar Gold Corp. in Venezuela; Eldorado Gold Corp. in Turkey; Gabriel Resources Ltd. in Romania; and Iamgold Corp. in West Africa to name a few.

It's still too early to know if they're going to run into any problems, but based on the experiences of other projects overseas, the odds are that they will face at least one hurdle before they extract any gold.

Gold mining overseas means companies often have to cope with a plethora of issues that their operations in Canada don't have to contend with, such as:

• Lack of basic infrastructure—companies have to factor in the costs of building accommodation for workers, and obtaining access to electrical power and water supply, even in areas that aren't remote.

• Labour can be inexpensive, but chances are the workers need to be educated or trained in current mining techniques and procedures.

• Volatile political climate—the government officials that the company negotiates with are routinely voted out of office...or worse.

So what does this mean for the investor? Should you avoid buying shares in companies that are exploring or producing gold overseas? Absolutely not. Acknowledge that the risks are bigger and therefore the investment analysis needs to be more thorough. However, the potential rewards associated with owning exploration companies that successfully mine gold overseas are substantial.

Buying Signals
Things are looking promising in the gold sector these days, primarily because the forecast for the price of gold is better than it's been in decades. Senior producers and more junior companies have the financing they need to explore or acquire.

Buying stocks in a senior gold producing company is as much of a "sure thing" as you can get in the resource sector simply because the price of gold is climbing and should continue to climb based on financial market conditions and low supply.

Buying shares in junior and intermediate companies offers greater potential returns, but at the same time, involves tolerating a greater level of risk. You can mitigate the risks to a significant degree by diversifying your portfolio. Buy a variety of the exploration companies with good prospects, but also include mid-tier or intermediate producers that have a motivated and talented exploration team.

Factors to research and consider before buying shares in a junior, intermediate or senior gold company:

• *The Leaders*: Top of the list when checking out an investment prospect is always the quality of management. Examine the company Web site for the credentials, experience and accomplishments of the management team. Ask your investment advisor for similar information from their research department.

• *The Discoveries*: A pure exploration company will not be mining gold, have any revenues, or earnings. Look at their press releases to get an insight into their potential for success. The more drilling results they have, the better the deposit is defined geologically, and therefore, the lower the risk. One factor that isn't important is the quality of the grade of gold discovered. High-grade discoveries can prove to be disappointing if the deposit isn't large enough, while lower grades can be lucrative if the deposit is large and easily mined. Underground mining for gold is more difficult, extremely expensive and therefore not worth it unless the deposits are sufficiently large, e.g. Goldcorp's Red Lake mine. Open-pit mining, e.g. Northgate's Kemess Mines or Cumberland's Meadowbank Mine, is easier and therefore less costly to operate.

• *The Budgets*: An intermediate company will actually be producing gold, but revenues are usually plowed right back into the exploration budget. Concentrate on determining whether the money being re-invested is paying off. Good management will deploy their funds prudently in order to discover new reserves or improve upon existing mining operations. The transition from junior explorer (spending culture) to intermediate producer (balancing a budget) is not an easy one to make.

• *The Earnings*: A senior production company is like most other mature businesses. Successful ones are self-financing, with sufficient earnings to fund a reasonable exploration program. Unlike junior and intermediate companies that are forced to grow their reserves through exploration, the challenge of senior producers is to find replacements for their existing reserves as they naturally deplete. Growth for senior gold producing companies is more likely to occur through mergers and acquisitions.

• *The Takeovers*: A good omen that the market for gold was going to improve was the purchase of TVX Gold Inc. and Echo Bay Mines Ltd. by Kinross Gold Corp. in January of 2003. Kinross acquired the two troubled gold companies and expanded its reserves without dipping into its exploration budget. In retrospect, the timing was perfect and the acquisitions look remarkably inexpensive compared with today's going rates. The problem is that intermediate companies like Kinross experience many challenges as they endeavour to grow into seniors. The company's mines will be depleted within several years unless there are significant new discoveries or they make more acquisitions. Time will tell whether they will find a catalyst that takes them to the next level. While takeovers can be an indicator of growth and strength, they can also be the death knell for the market, as noted in the "signs to sell" section that follows.

RISK/RETURN ILLUSTRATION OF MAJORS, INTERMEDIATE
AND JUNIOR COMPANIES (fig. 6)

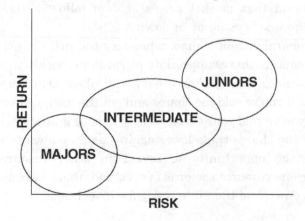

Signs to Sell

Warning signs that it's time for investors to sell include:

• As soon as newspaper and magazine headlines are riddled with stories on the price of gold, or gold companies and the lifestyles of their executives, then it's time to get worried. As difficult as it is to unload a winning stock, it's always time to sell when the market is hot.

• If people who know less than you about investing or mining start offering you tips on which gold stocks you should buy, then it's likely the sector is approaching a peak. Chances are that the gold price and the prices of gold company shares have already risen a lot, so the odds of them continuing to rise are getting slim. The real kicker? If you feel the urge to start gloating about how much your own portfolio of gold stocks has skyrocketed, squelch it and sell.

• When there's a lot of takeover and merger activity at premium prices then it's time to sell. The premium over the market price that one company is willing to pay to buy another is usually relatively low at a market bottom, when takeover premiums can range from 10% to 20% more than the quoted share price. On the other hand, the premium can be quite high at a market peak, often in the neighborhood of 30% to 50% more than the market price. If takeover activity becomes fast and furious, with senior producers acquiring lots of junior companies at sizable markups, it's time to stop investing in gold stocks.

A great deal of evidence suggests that gold bullion and gold company stocks are in the early stages of a sustainable rally that could last several years. However, it's important for every investor to keep in mind that market prices seldom follow a straight line, whether the line is going up or down.

As a general rule of thumb, whenever the price of gold and the price of company shares appreciate in value so quickly that it seems a little ridiculous, then chances are it is ridiculous. Don't forget, it's not a profit until you've sold the shares and got the money in your pocket.

When you've sold your stocks to lock in your gains, you can either wait until the shares trade lower again—as they always do—or you can take the opportunity to invest in other resource stocks. Whenever one resource sector is overvalued, there's always another one that's down and therefore ready for investment.

CHAPTER FIVE

Base Metals

Mining for metals and minerals doesn't have the same romantic lure as diamonds or gold, but the prospective returns for investors in this sub-sector could be downright racy. Traces of non-precious metals such as nickel or copper are found in nearly every manufactured item—from the guitar strings that snap during an overly-energetic set, to the cell phones that rock stars use to call their agents, to the wire in the bras thrown on stage by their groupies.

A great example of the prevalence of base metals in everyday objects is your car. It's made up of umpteen metals—steel, nickel, aluminum and copper, to name a few—most of which are cleverly concealed behind plastic trim. The catalytic converter that converts toxic fumes into harmless air and water is made out of a unique metal called palladium.

We tend to take the things made from metals for granted, and most of us could care less where they come from. After all, the metals seem to be in abundant supply. But we should care, because when there's a shortage, we all pay.

The earth is indeed chock full of the basic metals that manufacturers need in order to crank out all the items that their customers demand. The catch is getting as much as they need—and even more importantly, getting it when they need it—to produce items like cars.

Deposits of nickel, copper, iron ore and other metals are scattered around the world, but finding and then digging them out of the earth requires both capital and ingenuity.

Making matters even more complicated is that the demands of manufacturers are erratic. For example, if cars are selling at an exceptionally fast rate, then automobile producers are going to need a lot of metals to produce enough to meet the demand. That's the start of a boom cycle. As sales slow down, manufacturers will cut back on production and therefore won't need as much metal. That's when the mining sector starts to feel the pinch and a different cycle begins.

Every economic cycle has its own dynamics, which in turn influences the demand and supply for a variety of materials all in different ways. Understanding the cycles is the key to knowing when it's a good time to invest in mining companies. This chapter will identify the important data and patterns that should help you make money from investing in base metals.

Driving the Cycles
An economic cycle is driven by the demands for all basic materials. For example, when automobile sales are up, manufacturers order more of the metals that they'll need to build more cars, such as copper for wiring, stainless or galvanized steel (which is made up of nickel and zinc), and palladium for the catalytic converters. If there's a surplus of these metals in the inventories of mining companies around the world, then it's unlikely that the prices of the base metals will be affected very much by the surge in demand.

If there's a shortage of the metals, then it's a good bet that the price of the metals, known as commodities, will rise. There's no way that major car manufacturers will refuse to build and deliver new models just because there's a shortage of copper or nickel. The profits are too big (plus they can pass on some, if not all of the higher costs of production to the consumer), and shutting down assembly lines would cost millions of dollars.

The key factor in investing in metals is to understand what's happening in the economy on a big scale. For example, a booming economy plus low interest rates usually creates a greater demand for cars, which subsequently increases the need for more base metals. If that makes sense to you, then you're capable of successfully investing in base metals.

Consider the global economic trends and their impact on base-metal producers. For example, China is one of the driving forces behind the growing world economy, both literally and figuratively. Not only does China have one of the fastest growing GDPs but in 2002, car sales in China rose by 55% to over a million vehicles sold. Sales shot up again in 2003. More than one hundred million Chinese earn over $5,000 annually, which is considered the threshold for automotive purchases. That's why Peugeot-Citroën, General Motors Corp., Ford Motor Co., DaimlerChrysler AG, Toyota Motor Co., Fiat, Renault-Nissan, BMW, Hyundai Motor Co. and Honda have all built assembly operations in China.

As a result, industrial spinoff manufacturers are also setting up shop. A case in point is that China is now an exporter of auto parts. This is great news for the mining sector, as it will have to meet both international and domestic demands. Chinese auto parts manufacturers will need to import a lot of the base metals to manufacture the parts for domestic use and for export. Simultaneously, increased sales of automobiles in China will fuel the demand for the same metals that manufacturers in other countries will need to make the products that are exported to China. It's one giant cycle—and this is only in the automotive industry. Think of all the metal needed to produce the other items in demand by consumers in a booming economy and you get an idea of why the market for base metals is going to take off in the next few years.

Sourcing the Supply
As lesser-developed countries build the infrastructure (roads, buildings, telecommunications networks, etc.) that are necessary if they are going to compete in a global marketplace, then demand for basic materials will continue to increase at an alarming rate. The big question is then about supply: Are there enough of these metals to meet demand?

U.S. NON-FERROUS METAL PRODUCT INVENTORIES,1982-2003, US$B,
(fig. 7)

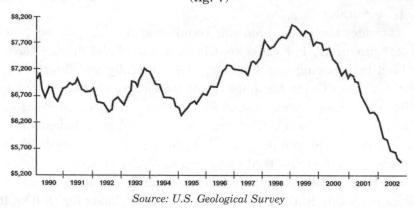

Source: U.S. Geological Survey

As discussed in earlier chapters, the tech bubble didn't have a positive impact on the resources market. For the most part, basic industries in general and base metals in particular have been in a financial slump for decades. The lack of demand for base metals resulted in reduced exploration and mine development, which had the ultimate effect of shrinking the inventories at metal-producing companies.

Over the past year, the prices of nickel and copper—two metals that are extremely sensitive to changes in the economy—have been rising steadily as global demand for them began to increase. Not all metals are created equal, however. The seemingly insatiable appetite for stainless steel in Asia in the last few years depleted the supply of nickel to the point where chronic shortages will likely be the norm for the next few years.

The problem is that there's no end in sight to the shortage of nickel. New world-class deposits are at the earliest stages of development and it will take years before any of them can produce a significant and steady supply of nickel.

One of the best-known deposits is Voisey's Bay in Newfoundland, which was bought by Inco Ltd. in 1996. After six years of painstaking negotiations between Inco and the provincial government, it's still going to take the company years of work before any ore sees the light of day. Current expectations are that full commercial production will commence in 2011...fifteen years after they bought the ore body. At the same time, Inco's Goro nickel reserve in New Caledonia, one of the largest islands in the Pacific Ocean, is plagued by cost overruns and delays.

NICKEL PRICES AND INVENTORIES (fig. 8)

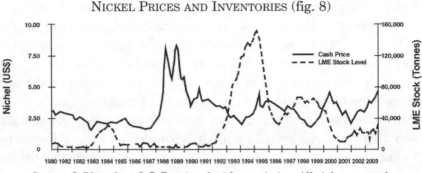

Limited supply and growing demand means that the price of nickel will continue to climb steadily as long as inventories are diminishing. As a result, the shares of nickel producers should do quite well early in this coming economic boom. Small exploration companies that find or develop nickel will also benefit.

Spotting Trends
Savvy investors try to identify trends before they occur. The best time to buy the stocks of major nickel producers, like Inco or Falconbridge Ltd., is just before supplies are diminished and prices start to rise. Conversely, when there's not such a strong demand for nickel by manufacturers or builders—and there's plenty of it on hand if they do need it—then the shares in nickel producers should be cheap.

As the price for nickel on the open market climbs, then mining companies are motivated to increase their exploration budgets, ramp up production on existing mines, and rebuild their decimated inventories.

Resources are called "cyclical" for a good reason. If rising demand and a chronic lack of supply is going to drag on for years, then it's still a good time to buy shares in mining companies even if they've already experienced a significant rally. The top producers will make money because they're selling a product that has a limited supply for a great price. Selling even more nickel at a higher price will increase both revenues and profits.

The time to worry is when evidence of the next economic slowdown starts to appear. When you see the cycle start to shift gears and go into reverse, it's time to sell your mining stocks.

For example, if people get insecure about their jobs, then they're unlikely to buy a new car. This decreased demand will mean cars won't move off the lots as fast as they used to so dealers will start cutting prices to reduce their inventory. If the cars still don't sell despite the lower price, then things start to get ugly. Manufacturers slow down their production lines, cut back on buying base metals, and mining companies take a hit. Their revenues drop, followed by a slump in the price of their shares, and voila, a perfect time for the canny investor to buy.

If you buy shares when the situation is looking ugly, and sell when things are rosiest, then there are good returns to be earned from investing in resource stocks.

Not All the Same

A key point to remember, though, is that not all metals operate on the same cycles. Take copper, for example. Unlike nickel, there's plenty of copper in inventories to satisfy the growing demands of manufacturers.

COPPER PRICES AND INVENTORIES (fig. 9)

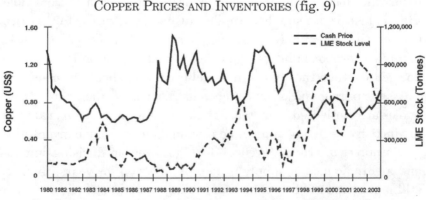

Source: © Bloomberg L.P. Reprinted with permission. All rights reserved. Visit www.Bloomberg.com.

Even so, it's not unusual for the price of a metal like copper to begin rising despite the fact that there's tons in the inventories held by mining companies. The prices will start to climb because of the moves made by professional commodity traders. When they see more copper being used, they begin buying it in the futures markets (where they don't have to pay for it until later on). They're counting on the fact that if manufacturers are using more copper, then at some point the inventories will diminish, and then prices will start to rise.

As you can see from the chart above, it's estimated that inventories—although plentiful in 2002 and 2003—are poised to decline. That bodes well for an increase in the price of copper. If the global economy continues to grow as expected, then companies that supply copper will eventually benefit from the trend, even though it will take them longer to reap the rewards being enjoyed by major nickel producers right now.

Major Decisions
Once you understand the trends and have learned to spot the right timing in the economic cycles, then which metal producers are the best ones to invest in? Does it make sense to invest only in the major producers? Or should you buy shares in junior and intermediate companies? The key issues presented in the previous chapter on investing in gold producers are just as relevant when it comes to investing in more cyclical metals.

The more conservative approach is to invest in globally competitive companies whose fortunes are linked to the commodity. Inco is usually a first choice when you're considering buying shares in nickel producers. It controls the lion's share of the world nickel market because it owns the largest producing mines as well as the most prospective sources of nickel.

The other major Canadian player is Falconbridge Ltd. Its financial success is primarily dependent on rising nickel prices, but because it is more diversified than Inco (it also mines copper and zinc) it is affected by the prices of other metals. So even if nickel prices are rising faster than floodwaters on a rainy day, low prices in other metal markets could mean that Falconbridge would still be struggling to keep its head above water.

Another major player to consider is Teck Cominco Ltd. as it also produces a diversified mix of metals: copper, zinc and gold.

The aluminum market has been improving, in which case Alcan Inc. is your best bet even though Alcoa in the U.S. offers the same opportunities for investors.

ALUMINUM PRICES AND INVENTORIES (fig. 10)

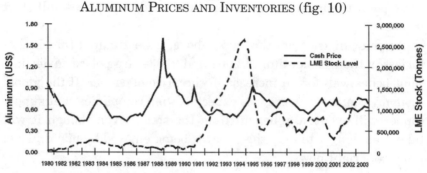

Source: © Bloomberg L.P. Reprinted with permission. All rights reserved.
Visit www.Bloomberg.com.

As long as interest rates remain low worldwide to fuel economic growth, and countries continue spending money on major infrastructure projects, then there will be a cyclical boom in base metals and other raw materials in the next few years. That's why investors should include base-metal stocks in their portfolios more than ever before. Which of the major producers you decide to invest in will depend on your gut feeling about which metal prices will move up the most aggressively, and when you expect them to move. Nickel prices are already rising at press time, but it's becoming increasingly apparent that soon copper prices will follow suit. Eventually even the prices paid for zinc will start to move up.

Overseas Discoveries
Once the prices paid for base metals starts to improve, then you'll usually see the same pattern that happens in the gold sector. Larger companies, because of their shareholders, are under pressure to increase their revenues. When times are tough—and for the last two

decades, times have been tough for metal producers—major companies are forced to cut back on their expenditures. The first and easiest cost to cut back on is exploration programs. After all, why spend scarce dollars exploring for metals, when your customers aren't buying what you've already got on hand?

There's also a culture that evolves in larger corporations that discourages any exploration activity that will only have a negligible impact. For example, a geologist may find a new copper deposit, but initial drilling results indicate it's only a twenty million ton resource. Head office might have a one hundred million ton cut-off as anything smaller won't have a big enough impact on the company's bottom line. Frustrated, the geologist moves on to other projects (some even leave to form their own exploration company) and the deposit gets lost in the company files.

When copper demand picks up and its price starts to rise, senior management will likely just buy a company that has already developed a one hundred million ton resource, and fold that operation into their own. Alcan's purchase of the French industrial group Pechiney in 2003 is a prime example of how large resource companies continue to grow.

This pattern of "big fish eat small fish," is a recurring theme in natural resource industries. It represents a wealth of opportunities for investors, mainly because what's garbage for some is profitable for others.

A good example of this is the work being done in Africa by First Quantum Minerals Ltd., a Vancouver-based team of opportunistic and entrepreneurial engineers, many of whom were frustrated by the limits imposed on them when they worked for major producers. Because they're a small and creative outfit, they're in a prime position to exploit the scrap mines abandoned by the big companies.

Over the years, they've managed to create some successful operations by combining raw determination with modern exploration and mining techniques. Major producers are often handcuffed by their "go big or go home" approach to projects, while highly motivated geochemists, geologists and engineers will "just do it" and come up with a way to make it profitable.

Several years ago, the management team at First Quantum

Minerals, spearheaded by Philip Pascall, chairman, and Clive Newall, president, unearthed an opportunity in Zambia. The Zambian Copperbelt has been around for ages and had been picked over many times by most of the majors. One copper mine, Bwana Mkubwa (Big Boss), was mined from the early 1900s to 1984 when it was considered "mined out." In 1996, First Quantum acquired the mining lease by staking a claim on the leftover deposits. The company proceeded to run these leftovers (called "tailings" in the industry, considered the garbage of the industry) through the processing plant. They discovered that there's enough copper in the tailings to keep operations running for at least five years.

Ambitiously, they subsequently explored and discovered a new deposit, Lonshi, just on the other side of the Zambian/Congo border. Ore from this new mine is already being converted into sheets of cathode copper (which refers to the way the copper is made as well as the way it is sold). Then First Quantum announced in September 2003 that it discovered another new deposit, Lufua, in the Democratic Republic of Congo.

Sometimes junior and intermediate producers get lucky with their projects. Again, First Quantum is a good example. Back in 1997, Cyprus Amax Minerals Co., which was later acquired by the American mining monolith Phelps Dodge Corp., bought the majority of Kansanshi, one of the oldest mines in Zambia (there's evidence that copper smelting at the mine dates back to the fourth century). After completing some eighty thousand meters of exploration drilling and a feasibility study that didn't meet their investment criteria, Phelps Dodge abandoned the project.

First Quantum acquired an 80% interest in the mine in 2001. Since all the really expensive exploration work was already done, it was then just a matter of applying some effective, but low-cost mining ingenuity—something that Canadian and Australian mining companies are famous for—to churn out the copper.

Applying modern exploration techniques with mining ingenuity in areas where the major companies can't be bothered to explore can prove to be extremely successful. Investors who are willing to do a little extra homework on the projects underway at junior and inter-mediate companies may find themselves enjoying the rewards of owning a winner on two accounts: a producer when the outlook for copper is improving; and a company that's improving its bottom line by growing its reserves and increasing production.

FIRST QUANTUM STOCK PRICE APRIL TO SEPTEMBER 2003 (fig. 11)

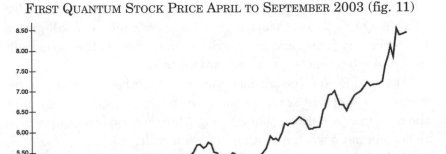

Success at Home

You don't have to travel overseas to find all the great mining stories. FNX Mining Company Inc. is a junior mining company that's making it big in Canada.

In January 2002, FNX took out an option on five of Inco's former producing properties in the Sudbury Basin. Terry MacGibbon, president and CEO of FNX, worked as an exploration geologist with Inco for thirty years. While Inco's senior management was hunting for the next big deposit in Labrador and around the world, MacGibbon believed there was still a lot of potential closer to home. After all, the best place to look for metals is where you know they exist, and the Sudbury area has long been the source of some of Canada's most lucrative mining deposits. Since FNX optioned the former Inco properties, it has been conducting one of the world's largest exploration programs in a well-established mining camp.

The company has enjoyed tremendous exploration success by employing modern geological and geophysical techniques, 3D computer modeling, and has attracted a skilled and dedicated team.

FNX began production in 2003, partnered with Dynatec Corp., their joint venture partner and mining operator.

As is the case in the gold sector, investing in junior and intermediate companies is riskier than buying shares in the majors, but the odds of a greater reward are there if you bet on the right ones. Just as a rising tide lifts all boats, a global economic recovery will give a boost to many junior and intermediate companies at the same time that senior base-metal producers are profiting.

The onus is on investors, however, to do their best to separate the companies that will survive and thrive during a global boom from the ones that will drown while trying. Here are the basic guidelines to keep in mind when investing in base metals:

• The best time to buy cyclical stocks—and base metals are definitely cyclical—is when nobody is recommending that you buy them.

• Although a global economic recovery can lead to several years of prosperity for metal producers, the end of the boom will eventually come. Keep in mind these key factors: When the price of the commodity is strong, more money and energy will be devoted to discovering new deposits. As more metal is produced and brought to market then inventory levels will rise. If supply is greater than the demand for the metal, then the cycle is about to reverse.

Stocks are generally one step ahead of the industry, so watch for the first signs that a downturn is about to happen in the sector. Unfortunately, the signs are not all that easy to identify. There's only talk of a recession or an economic downturn in the media when we're already in the middle of one. Long before that point, cyclical stocks will already be spiraling downwards.

The right time to sell cyclical stocks in general—and the shares of base-metal companies in particular—is when everyone is telling you to buy them. Keep an eye on the prices of the individual commodities and watch for any signs of them slowing down or inventory levels starting to rise over historical norms. That's really the only way that investors can take their profits and exit before the party's over.

Research from your investment advisor is a great source of data, but be careful to distinguish between the facts and the recommendations. On average, research analysts are notoriously bad at timing their buy/sell recommendations in these sectors, but their reports do contain a wealth of information that you can use to understand the trends in these cyclical sectors.

CHAPTER SIX
Oil and Gas

Energy is one resource that has been smokin' hot for investors in the past few years, but by the end of 2003 it was time for people to dampen their enthusiasm for buying shares in oil and gas companies.

Because of the explosive combination of increased demand and limited supply, energy companies have seen the price of their shares rise in tandem with the escalating prices paid for oil and gas. Prices hit a twenty-year low in 1999 then rose steadily for the next few years. Yet investors need to know that the energy sector goes through short economic cycles and should understand that a quick downturn in the market can result in some serious burns.

The good news is that because the energy sector does go through such short cycles, then even when it is in a downward spiral, it's usually not long before it pulls out of the slump. That's when there's a lot of opportunities to pump up the volume of your investment in this industry.

Fueling Prices
Unlike other resources, most consumers are acutely aware of pricing in the oil and gas market—at least for the final product. We're reminded on almost daily basis of the fluctuations that are an inherent hallmark of this volatile sector. Probably the best example was in

the summer of 2003 when most drivers succumbed to sticker shock as the price of gas skyrocketed.

Sticker shock and panic are standard sentiments driving investors and consumers when it comes to the oil and gas sector. The root of many of their worries can be traced back to when The Club of Rome (a non-profit, non-governmental organization made up of scientists, economists, entrepreneurs, senior civil servants, as well as current and former heads of state from around the world) published a study in 1972 called *The Limits to Growth*. The controversial book predicted that if the world's consumption patterns and population growth continued at the same high rates of growth at the time, then the earth would run out of resources like oil. The study shocked environmentalists and enraged economists.

These days, fear of running out of oil and gas is not at the fore-front of investor concerns, although it is still a key point. Price is much more of a major issue. Most investors tend to adhere to the philosophies of Adam Smith, an eighteenth century political econo-mist who believed that the market was self-equilibrating. Smith maintained that price has a major influence on consumer behaviour. If goods become too expensive, then demand will decrease. Conversely, if there's too much of a particular product available in a market, then producers will cut prices in order to stimulate sales.

In the short term, pricing doesn't have that much of an impact on consumption as oil and gas are staples in our society. People grudg-ingly pay the higher prices, while companies pass on the increased fuel costs to their customers.

Suppliers have us almost literally "over a barrel" as most modes of transportation require fuel of one type or another—diesel, gaso-line, propane, oil, natural gas, you name it. No matter what the final form is, all fuel is drawn from reservoirs of fossil fuels buried deep within the earth. (They're called "fossil fuels" because they originated with prehistoric plants and animals that used to live in the lakes and oceans. Glacial sediment covered the bodies of water, burying the decomposing animals and plants. Centuries later, this matter changed into liquids that can be extracted, processed, then pumped as fuel into machines.)

Short Economic Cycles

The graph below illustrates the short cyclical nature of the price of West Texas Intermediate, one of the most commonly used benchmarks for the price of crude oil. It climbed substantially from a low in 1998 to a high of US$37.83 per barrel on March 12th, 2003. Prices peaked during the Iraq War in the spring of that year.

SHORT OIL CYCLES (fig. 12)

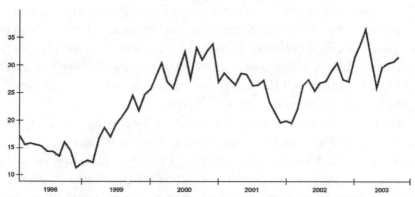

Source: © Bloomberg L.P. Reprinted with permission. All rights reserved.
Visit www.Bloomberg.com.

A spike is typical in this sector whenever there are hostilities in the Middle East, the source of most of the world's oil supply. If investors are worried about a disruption in supply, there is usually a speculative surge in the price of crude oil.

It all boils down to the politics of oil, a subject that's as volatile as the resource it's based on. The key player is OPEC, the Organization of the Petroleum Exporting Countries. Founded in Iraq in 1960, today it has eleven members: Algeria, Indonesia, Iran, Iraq, Kuwait, Libya, Nigeria, Qatar, Saudi Arabia, the United Arab Emirates and Venezuela. Since OPEC accounts for roughly 40% of the world's oil production, and its member countries sit on two-thirds of all proven crude oil reserves, then any disruption in the supply from OPEC producers can have staggering repercussions.

Although most people think that OPEC's mission is to control the price of oil on world markets, this is not the case. One of the most basic economic calculations is that price multiplied by quantity sold equals total revenue. OPEC uses its firm grip on supply to influence oil prices and subsequently earn the highest profits possible. It's only logical that OPEC leaders want to optimize their revenues and the best way to do that is not to insist on a steady price, but rather to set a price that maximizes total revenues even as demand for the product fluctuates. Consequently, the price of oil always has been—and always will be—volatile.

This volatility also comes from the fact that the economic cycle of the oil and gas sector is different from the cycles of other natural resources. It's a short round trip from market peak to trough, largely because the supply of fossil fuels can be turned on or off relatively quickly. Saudi Arabia alone controls more than 30% of the total OPEC production so if the world demands more oil, they can almost quite literally turn on the tap and deliver it.

As with most other natural resources, volatility can be a bane to investors, or it can be their best friend. Even more challenging for investors is that the fortunes of the oil and gas industry are also complicated by the availability of alternative sources of energy, whether from coal, hydro, solar or even nuclear power. When the price of oil is too high, for example, some heavy users switch to these alternative energy sources.

Increased Demand

Most investors taking a look at the graph above, and considering the steady climb of the price of crude oil until late 2003, would conclude that investing in oil and gas companies is a great idea. Human nature being what it is means that most people want to jump in while the market is hot. After having read the earlier chapters in this book, you'll know that this is a warning that the market is about to enter a downward cycle—maybe not right away, but definitely in the near future.

Because demand for this widely used resource shows no sign of slowing down and inventories of oil and gas are way below normal levels, companies have been pouring money into exploration projects in hopes of finding the next big reserve. The good news is that, unlike metals and minerals, fossil fuels can usually be discovered rather quickly and relatively inexpensively. On the other hand, it's getting more difficult to find new sources, especially of natural gas.

The energy sector has enjoyed a long bull market that is close to being the most sustained boom since the 1970s. Then shouldn't a global economic recovery mean that the demand for energy would continue to rise? The answer is yes.

According to the Energy Information Administration's latest Short Term Energy Outlook, world demand is expected to grow by 1.3 million BOE/d (Barrels of Oil Equivalent per day) in both 2003 and 2004, to a total of 79.8 million BOE/d in 2004. Half of this growth is expected to come from China, and the other half from the U.S. These predictions could prove to be conservative if the global rebound turns out to be as robust as we've suggested it will be.

Why isn't it a good time right now to buy energy stocks? Simply because the higher prices of crude oil and natural gas in recent years will inevitably change the supply available. Just like the hog farmer who wants to breed and sell more hogs in a hot market for pork bellies, oil and gas producers hope to take advantage of high prices by boosting production. As a result, international drilling activity in 2003 was at its highest level in the past five years. When the contents of the newly discovered reserves hit the market, demand will be satisfied, inventories will be rebuilt, and then prices will start to decline.

Crude Politics

A wild card in the whole equation is the remaining 60% of the world's oil supply that comes from the U.S., Canada, Russia and a host of other non-OPEC countries. Large integrated oil and gas producers in Canada such as Imperial Oil Ltd. and Shell Canada Ltd. are divisions of multinational companies with operations in countries where there are large reserves.

Even Canadian companies with roots in the western sedimentary basin (the source of fossil fuels in our western provinces) such as Talisman Energy Inc., Nexen Inc., Canadian Natural Resources Ltd., EnCana Corp. and Suncor Energy Inc., have to varying degrees done business beyond our borders and become international oil and gas producers in the process.

Supply from these non-OPEC countries will soon be increasing, and if consumers and manufacturers are using less energy than the companies are processing, then producers are going to start lowering prices so they won't be stuck with large inventories. OPEC will try to compensate to some extent by decreasing their production levels in order to keep a lid on prices, but they will only go so far in terms of trying to control the market. Even OPEC countries are not foolish enough to risk losing their profits in order to help fill up the wallets of their global competitors.

OIL PRICE BULL MARKETS (fig. 13)
NYMEX 12 MONTH MOVING AVERAGES

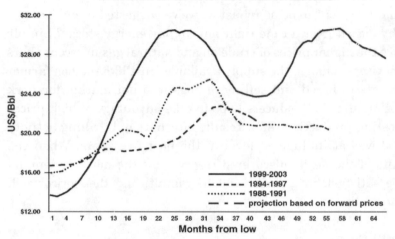

Source: Peters & Co. Ltd.

Patience and Discipline

Although this isn't the best time to invest in the energy sector, does that mean investors should stay away from it or ignore it altogether? Being a savvy investor in natural resources requires patience, and above all, discipline. Just because you don't own certain stocks at a given time does not mean you can stop doing your homework.

As the chart above shows, oil price bull markets last about three years on average. The subsequent bear markets don't last long either. The key is to stay aware of what's going on in the sector. Like a cat studying its prey, you want to be ready to pounce when the time is right.

The global demand for oil and gas will continue to climb in the next few years and energy companies will scramble to produce as much as they can. They'll pump out too much which will cause a temporary glut and prices will drop. Not until users consume the excess supply that will be available in the short term will prices start to rise. A good time to buy oil and gas stocks will be just before prices pull out of the slump and start to climb again.

Is it really worth it to do your homework? Consider this: From January 2002 to January 2003 (roughly when oil prices were at peak levels) the S&P/TSX 60 Energy Sub-Index total return was +15.90%. Compare this with the broader S&P/TSX 60 Index loss of –13.89% and you can see that patience and discipline can be well worth the effort. The prices of junior energy stocks rose on average in excess of 30% over this same time frame.

The catch is that *how* to invest in the oil and gas sector can sometimes be more challenging than *when*. The situation is constantly changing.

Major Pressure

In the past, a junior oil and gas company would hit the jackpot during exploration, pump out the reserves, and increase its production over time. With the financial support of well-rewarded investors, it would eventually become an intermediate oil and gas producer. Then a multinational company might acquire the company, or it could fend off takeover attempts and grow itself into an international contender with both upstream (exploration and production) and downstream (refining and marketing) operations.

This model is not that relevant these days. Larger companies have consolidated over the years and there are now fewer of them. As is the case with most other natural resource sectors, their sheer bulk prevents them from growing quickly. It's tough enough to find sufficient reserves to replace what they produce, refine it, and deliver it to market, let alone acquire productive juniors.

Shares in senior oil and gas producers rise and fall in tandem with commodity prices just like other cyclical resource industries, but the ups and downs are typically more volatile because of the reasons outlined above. Big oil and gas companies have been under such constant pressure to grow that they have virtually acquired all of the intermediate companies.

Larger companies with overseas operations have generally been successful discovering "black gold" in places like the North Sea, the Middle East, Africa, and even the Far East. Keep in mind the same risks of doing business overseas apply to companies in this sector as it does to their gold, diamond or base-metal peers.

Nexen (formerly Canadian Occidental Petroleum Ltd.), for example, has lucrative operations in Yemen. Historically a volatile country, several years ago it experienced a short revolution and investors panicked, pummeling the stock. This was a great buying opportunity, which wasn't much of a consolation for investors who succumbed to their fear and sold their stocks at a loss.

Talisman Energy faced quite a few hurdles with their interests in Sudan and, under intense public pressure, sold their 25% share in the Greater Nile Petroleum Operating Consortium in March 2003. Human rights activists protested that the income generated by the sale of oil from Sudan was being used to purchase arms and supplies for the government's side in the country's bloody civil war.

While there are risks of doing business overseas, it's sufficient to say that it's your responsibility as an investor to do enough research to know where companies have foreign operations and the corresponding political, environmental and legal risks of them doing business in those countries.

Royalty Trusts
The emergence of royalty trusts in Canada has also changed the face of investing in the energy sector. Structured differently than publicly traded corporations, they end up competing with oil and gas producers for both investment and reserves. Essentially, the trusts are large mutual funds, conceived as a means of owning mature oil and gas reserves.

Expenses related to exploration are tax deductible, so the government usually provides a variety of tax allowances to oil and gas companies to encourage them to invest more in exploration and development. The crunch comes when the companies eventually run out of tax breaks. When they do, they face a double whammy: taxes on their operations and taxes on the dividends paid to shareholders.

On the other hand, a layer of corporate taxation is avoided in a royalty trust as all the money earned from the trust's oil and gas operations flows directly through to the unitholders. Therefore, the earnings are only taxed when they get into the hands of the individual investors in the energy trust.

As a result of these favorable tax conditions, the popularity, number and size of royalty trusts has ballooned in recent years. In 2000, there were ten royalty trusts, with a combined market capitalization of $3.2 billion producing a total of 137,000 BOE/d (Barrels of Oil Equivalent per day). Three years later, there were twenty-two conventional oil and gas royalty trusts with a combined market capitalization of $19 billion, producing a total of 475,000 BOE/d. Many more will likely be created given their tremendous success.

Value and Production
Look closely, though, as there's something grossly wrong with this picture. The logic behind the structure of the royalty trust is quite compelling, but why has their "value" increased almost five times, while the combined production has only gone up two and a half times?

Investors are enamoured with the promise of a steady stream of distributions from royalty trusts, and for a variety of reasons many of the distributions even come with tax advantages. The problem is that people are only human and often they let greed overcome their better judgment. Investors love getting the generous dividends, but many seem blind to the fact that the high energy prices responsible for the current attractive yields won't stay high forever.

If oil and gas prices start to drop due to increasing supply, then the love affair between the investing public and royalty trusts will leave some investors with broken hearts. Distributions paid to unitholders will decline in tandem with decreasing energy prices, then disappointed investors will behave like lemmings and sell their units all at the same time which will erode the value of the shares even more.

Investors in natural resources should treat royalty trusts in the same way as other oil and gas stocks. If everybody owns the same trusts or company shares and absolutely loves them, then they should be avoided as an investment or sold. The unique structure of royalty trusts makes them a great way to invest in the sector, especially for more conservative investors. But remember that the time to buy them is when commodity prices are low and the unit prices are much lower than they were in 2003.

Junior Prospects

When the time is right to invest in the energy sector again, you should include some of the larger oil and gas companies in your portfolio, as well as some of the higher quality royalty trusts. However, the biggest bang for your buck is going to be an investment in junior exploration and production companies.

There are well over two hundred publicly traded oil and gas companies in Canada that would be classified as "small cap" (less than $1 billion in total outstanding shares). High commodity prices combined with the relatively high valuations in this sector have made it difficult to find undervalued companies, but the task will be less onerous in the near future when the price of oil and gas starts to drop.

Some of the more interesting junior companies are launched when creative and entrepreneurial professionals get fed up with the constraints of working for large, bureaucratic corporations and strike out on their own. Their upstart companies are often extremely successful and then subsequently acquired by larger companies or royalty trusts.

A recent phenomenon is the splitting of companies. The management teams hold on to their exploration properties and sell their producing wells and reserves in order to create a new junior exploration company. The producing properties are either spun off into a new energy trust or sold to an established royalty trust.

When the time is right to invest in the oil and gas sector, a number of the well-established but still junior companies would be a great place to start looking. For example, Cequel Energy Inc. is managed by the former team from Cypress Energy that was bought by PrimeWest Energy Trust in 2001. Since they took the helm at Cequel, the experienced crew has proven that they still have an innate ability to identify highly prospective properties, and to discover oil and gas reserves on those properties via the drill bit.

Rare Intermediates

Compton Petroleum Corp. began operations in 1993, which makes it one of the granddaddies of the junior/intermediate oil and gas companies. Not as aggressive as some of the other players in the Alberta energy patch, their strategy of consolidating interests in underdeveloped areas until they have a dominant position in land holdings and facilities is a tried-and-true approach. This has made them a veritable "steady Eddy" in the Canadian oil and gas industry.

Ketch Energy was a short-lived junior exploration success story. The team was so successful that they merged the company with Acclaim Energy Trust in 2002. Then Ketch Resources Ltd. was created to renew an exploration program on the properties of the former entity. Their subsequent drilling success has proven that this offspring has inherited the profitable characteristics of its parent company.

One of the most successful transformations began when Calpine Corp.(a large independent power producer in the U.S., but a perennial underperformer) acquired Encal Energy, one of the best managed intermediate companies in western Canada. After the 2001 takeover, the Encal management team moved to Progress Energy Ltd. and once again they're building value for their shareholders.

One of the few remaining intermediate oil and gas companies is Penn West Petroleum. The current team has been managing it since 1992 when the company was producing only 1,600 BOE/d. Ten years later, production exceeded 100,000 BOE/d. Given the speed with which successful intermediate companies are either acquired by large multinationals or converted into royalty trusts, it will be interesting to see how long Penn West remains in its current form.

Key Indicators

Hundreds of junior oil and gas exploration companies exist and a good many of them are worth investigating. Two key points to look for before investing in them are:

  • *Experienced Management*: motivated geologists and engineers who are extremely knowledgeable about the company's commodities and the geological formations that contain oil and gas usually ensure their companies are top performers.

• *Healthy Finances*: Watch out for companies that chronically spend far more on their exploration programs than they can afford. When commodity prices plummet, these operations run out of money and have to issue stock just to break even. When they flood the market with the additional batch of shares, your investment gets diluted. Ideally, a company's production growth rate should comfortably exceed the growth in the number of shares outstanding.

As with other resources, the best time to buy shares in exploration companies is when oil and gas prices have dropped. If a company is still increasing its reserves, production and cash flows in a hostile industry climate, then chances are they're an excellent growth company. They're your best bets for getting some seriously hot returns when the energy cycle starts to heat up again.

CHAPTER SEVEN
Coal

Lumps of coal in their shoes on St. Nicholas Day used to be the ultimate punishment for European children who had behaved badly during the year. Unfortunately for coal producers, they've been receiving more than their fair share of lumps because of bad global markets in the last two decades.

Warehouses are stockpiled with coal while the market continues to be battered by diminishing demand. This has dampened profitability for coal producers and cooled investor enthusiasm. In the summer of 2003, for example, coal traded at its lowest price in over twenty years on spot markets. (Also called a "cash market," a "spot market" is where commodities such as coal are bought and sold for cash and delivered immediately.)

Producers took some comfort from the fact that only 30% of the coal used for generating power is traded on spot markets. The vast majority of coal is sold under longer-term contracts, but even they have been concluded at extremely low rates.

Coal Deposits
People have been burning coal for more than four thousand years and it's played a major role in economic growth for centuries. It literally fueled the Industrial Revolution by producing the steam that powered the engines for factories, trains and ships.

These days, coal is second only to oil as a source of energy. It's burned to generate 40% of the world's electricity. Roughly 10% of global production is made into coke, a by-product that burns hotter and cleaner than coal, a quality valued by steel producers.

Countless coal deposits exist around the world, and there's enough of it to last several hundred years given current consumption rates. The leading producing countries include the U.S., China, Australia, India, South Africa, and Russia. There are also rich coal deposits all across Canada, making coal the single largest commodity transported by Canadian railways. The majority of Canadian coal is burned to produce electricity as coal-fired plants are the number one source of power generated by fossil fuels in the country.

Investing in Coal

The best time to invest in any natural resource is when the situation in the sector and the outlook for the commodity are at their bleakest. Using those guidelines, the timing is just about perfect to invest in Canadian coal producers because circumstances can't get much worse. After years of mining far more coal than the market needs, and burdened by the ensuing glut, many producers joined forces and consolidated their operations. Subsequent cost cutting has meant that the few remaining coal producers are on track to pick up steam, once the market turns around that is.

The only thing they need is for the world coal market to heat up. Looking at the chart below, if the global economy rebounds as it's expected to do in the next few years, then coal consumption could steadily increase. As consumption levels climb, existing inventories will gradually be depleted, and mines will then swing into production to meet the growing market demand. At that time, investors will likely rekindle their interest in coal producers. So if you're bullish on coal and optimistic about its prospects, then consider buying into the market before it starts to climb.

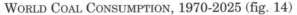

WORLD COAL CONSUMPTION, 1970-2025 (fig. 14)

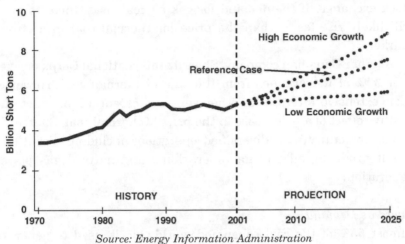

Source: Energy Information Administration

Canadian Market

Researching publicly traded coal producers is a relatively easy task. After the radical restructuring of the Canadian coal industry in early 2003, there are few producers left.

Canada's three leading exporters—Fording Inc., Luscar Ltd. and Teck Cominco Ltd.—merged their metallurgical coal assets (coal which is used to make coke for the steel industry) into a single company called Elk Valley Coal Corp. Elk Valley Coal is now 65% owned by the Fording Canadian Coal Trust and 35% by Teck Cominco and is the world's second largest producer of high-quality, export metallurgical coal.

Given the close links between coal consumption and steel production, it's a good sign for the coal industry that demand for steel in the Far East has been extremely strong. North American steel producers have had a tough time for many years, but with continued strong automobile sales as well as new pipelines and other infrastructure projects in the works, the market may also improve for them in the near future. This could give producers a chance to increase the price for coking coal.

Investors who believe the market for coking coal is going to improve should consider Fording Canadian Coal Trust. With operations in Canada, the U.S. and Mexico, the trust is structured differently than a typical corporation so units (instead of shares) are traded on the stock exchange. If the demand for coking coal rises, then its price will likely rise faster than the price for thermal coal in a strong market.

Another Canadian company, Sherritt International Corp., derives over 30% of its revenues from the sale of thermal coal. However, their extensive interests in other ventures essentially negates the positive effect of any increase in the price of thermal coal. Sherritt is a massive entity with diversified operations including nickel and cobalt products, oil and gas operations, and natural gas power generation.

Overseas Demand

Almost 55% of the coal consumed worldwide is used to generate electricity. It's logical then that the largest share of the projected increase in global coal consumption will likely be used for the same purpose. Look at where the largest increase in economic growth is likely to occur in order to forecast who will be the main consumers of electricity—and therefore coal—in the coming years. The answer? China and India.

In both countries, coal continues to be the main source of fuel. Given how rapidly their industrial sectors have been expanding and are projected to be growing, they will need a steady stream of coal to fuel their economic expansion. While China and India both possess major coal reserves, the rapid pace of their growth may force them to import coal in order to meet the urgent demands of their domestic markets.

Environmental Factors

While the market for coal is plagued with many issues, the largest and most unpredictable one is environmental. Coal mining has a direct impact on the environment in many ways: from the effect that mining has on the land, to management of mine waste. But by far the most significant issue affecting coal consumption is public concern about harmful emissions from burning coal. Carbon dioxide emissions per unit of energy from coal are significantly higher than those from burning other fuels for electricity generation.

The U.S. and China are the world's largest coal consumers. Although U.S. industries will likely cut back on burning coal because of public pressure to reduce carbon dioxide emissions, it's unlikely that environmental concerns will be an issue for China's current leaders. They seem to be focused on one thing and one thing only: fueling the rapid growth in their economy.

The environmental wild card is what makes investing in coal producers such a gamble these days. No one knows what the financial impact will be on the sector if current global initiatives to cutback on harmful emissions are successful. It's not that coal burning is going to be eliminated anytime soon. Instead, it's more a matter of estimating how much coal will be consumed, when, and where. Only when you understand all of the factors affecting Canada's beleaguered coal producers should a decision to invest be made.

Chapter Eight

Uranium

While all natural resources ignite a certain level of debate among their proponents and opponents, no other resource sparks as many heated discussions as uranium and its use in nuclear reactors.

Advocates argue that nuclear energy is a clean, cost-efficient source of power because it doesn't emit greenhouse gases. They maintain it is much better for the environment than its fossil fuel alternatives and is responsible for lowering the number of deaths due to respiratory illness.

Opponents merely mention one word: Chernobyl. The world's worst nuclear accident occurred in 1986 when an uncontrolled power increase destroyed the core of a nuclear reactor in the Ukraine, dispersing radioactive contaminants across a wide region in the former Soviet Union.

Regardless of which side of the issue you're on, it's wise to know the facts about uranium, many of which will come as a complete surprise to the average investor. Few people seem to know that the world's largest uranium producer is a publicly traded Canadian company, or that the second largest known reserves of uranium in the world are found in northern Saskatchewan. Australia has more uranium than any other country (28% of the world's known reserves), but for a variety of reasons—namely high-quality and low-cost production—Canada, with 15% of the known reserves, is the dominant supplier of uranium to world markets.

Another surprising fact is that most of the world's nuclear reactors are concentrated on the east coast of the U.S., Japan, and in Europe, the stronghold of the global environmentalist movement. Certain countries are extremely dependent on nuclear power: in France 75% of its electrical output was generated by nuclear reactors in 2000.

Chain Reaction

Uranium was officially discovered in 1789 by German chemist Martin Klaproth. He named the unusual element after the planet Uranus, which was discovered around the same time. Archaeologists unearthed glass containing uranium—with its characteristic fluorescent hues of yellow and green—dating as far back as AD 79.

Uranium is the heaviest of all naturally occurring elements, and as a result is used in the keels of yachts and aircraft rudders as counterweights. Uranium's notoriety, however, stems from its radioactive property, and how scientists have harnessed this rather complex energy source.

Uranium is found in rock, usually hundreds of meters below the surface of the earth. If left untouched, uranium decays slowly. But this radioactive element can also be extracted and split into smaller atoms, releasing a tremendous amount of energy in the process.

How does it work? In simple terms, neutrons are released during a splitting process called nuclear fission. These neutrons then come into contact with atoms, a process which in turn releases more neutrons, which can then "hit" more atoms, and so on. When this "splitting and hitting" activity is sustained it is called a nuclear chain reaction. The tremendous heat produced during a nuclear chain reaction inside a nuclear reactor is used to boil water. Steam then rises from the boiling water and turns the turbines. Voila, electricity is generated.

Incredible Growth

After Chernobyl, many people believed that environmentalists would ensure the plug was pulled on the nuclear power industry.

Instead, the role of nuclear power has strengthened considerably in the last decade.

Today, roughly one-fifth of the world's electricity is generated by over four hundred nuclear reactors. As the global appetite for energy continues to grow unabated, existing reactors increase their operating levels. Even Europe is rethinking the phasing out of nuclear reactors because of the difficulty in finding a replacement energy source that meets its requirements for reducing harmful emissions.

More than twenty-three nuclear reactors are currently under construction, three of which are scheduled to be up and running in China by 2005. Fourteen new ones are in the planning stage.

Given the continued proliferation of nuclear power stations, the prospects for uranium producers are good. Whenever demand outstrips supply, power plants are forced to buy excess inventory from producers as well as other consumers. If demand continues at the current rate, then existing uranium inventories could be eliminated in the near future.

Canadian Prospects

Even though the majority of uranium sales are made to power stations beyond our borders, the world's largest supplier is a Canadian company. Created in 1988 with the privatization of two Canadian crown corporations, Saskatchewan Mining Development Corp. and Eldorado Nuclear Ltd., Cameco Corp. is one of the lowest-cost producers. Uranium from Cameco mines fuel 20% of the nuclear reactors in the western world.

Cameco has a somewhat diversified range of operations including gold mining, diamond exploration, and shares in a nuclear power plant. The company owns 31.6% of Bruce Power LP, a consortium that leases eight nuclear reactors in Ontario and operates four of them. Cameco also has interests in an operating gold mine in Kyrgyzstan in central Asia, and a controlling interest in the Boroo gold mine project in northern Mongolia.

Cameco dominates the global uranium market, but a few smaller Canadian players are starting to make inroads in the sector. Southern Cross Resources Inc. is currently exploring and developing uranium mining properties, primarily in southern Australia.

In 2002, Cameco helped to establish a junior exploration company, UEX Corp. and retained a 35.5% stake in the newcomer. UEX is working with Cameco on uranium exploration in the Athabasca Basin area of northern Saskatchewan, the most important uranium-producing district in the world.

Future Forecast
Given the large amount of time that it takes to discover uranium deposits and develop new mines, and considering the increase in consumption by nuclear power stations, there could be a shortage of high-grade uranium unless the juniors manage to unearth new reserves.

New sources of uranium are likely to be found in Canada, Australia, the U.S., and central Asian republics. To date, all the other deposits have produced uranium that is of a much lower grade than the mines in Canada's Athabasca Basin. If the new sources are also lower grade, then they will be expensive to produce and process, a factor that could also cause the price of uranium to rise over the next few years. That would be good news for Cameco, as it sits comfortably on the highest-grade, lowest-cost, uranium deposit in the world.

Chapter Nine

Paper and Forestry Products

Oil and gas is a highly combustible industry, but the forestry sector has burnt more than its share of investors because of its volatile nature. As you can see from the chart below, lumber prices have behaved like a roller-coaster ride in the last two decades.

Slowly and steadily, lumber prices climbed to a peak in the early 1990s, followed by two rollicking good rides with plenty of hair-raising ups and downs. By the end of 2003, the ride slowed down, as if heading to the off-loading ramp. Nobody's been having fun lately…just seeing lots of depressing returns.

In many respects, the analogy is apt. By 2004, most investors in the forestry sector have probably headed for the exit. The question then is whether or not you should consider getting on for the next ride?

LUMBER PRICES FROM 1987 TO 2003 (fig. 15)

Eroding Strength

The industry has suffered a long streak of bad luck in the last few decades. Back in the 1980s, office communication switched from inter-office memos (remember those ubiquitous gold envelopes that could take weeks to make the rounds?) to an early form of the e-mail now in widespread use today. Since then, there's been a constant eroding of the print media by the electronic media. Subsequently, the worldwide purchases of pulp—the key component of every type of paper ranging from your morning newspaper to high-quality letter-head—have taken a beating.

The only good news for the forestry sector in the last twenty years has been a strong and steady demand for lumber for residential housing construction. But the strength in that market has been overshadowed by the downturn in demand for other forestry products such as newsprint. Because the majority of publicly traded paper and forest products companies produce a huge range of end products, the profits they make from increased sales in one market can be depleted by losses in another market.

The historical lumber price chart is almost the inverse of an energy prices chart: falling as fast as the prices of oil and gas rose. Looking at that gut-wrenching free fall makes it hard to envision how people can stomach investing in this sector again. However, this is precisely when paper and wood stocks are the most appealing to professional money managers as they whet their appetite for profits when the market rebounds.

No matter what investment analysis is used, almost everyone agrees that shares in forestry companies were cheap at the end of 2003. Of course, they're inexpensive for a good reason. In this sector, these companies have been bleeding money for years, but have managed to survive. They're the walking wounded and the odds are they'll be running at full strength one day.

Down-and-Out

Turn to the bond-rating services for a good indicator of how down-and-out a resource stock can get. Typically, these ratings are lagging, not leading, indicators. For example, in September 2003, Moody's Investors Service lowered the ratings of Tembec Inc. They said the downgrade reflected "the company's weakened performance as a result of low newsprint and lumber pricing, the adverse impact of a strengthened Canadian dollar on cash generation, and the limited prospects for a meaningful near-term recovery."

If it seems like nothing else could possibly go wrong for a forestry company and fundamentally they're a solid company with a good management team, then it's time to start thinking about what could go right. If you think that *anything* at all could change for the better, then it's time to consider investing in the sector once again.

The forestry products sector is a great example of a downtrodden opportunity. Investors throughout all the major stock markets have trivialized the sector. Paper and forest products companies account for a negligible 0.6% of the Standard & Poor 500 Index (the American stock market barometer which measures the value of five hundred major stocks). North of the border, these companies account for less than 2% of the total value of the Canadian equity market.

Time to Buy

As noted in earlier chapters, when natural resource sectors are extremely out-of-favor, there are great opportunities for people to make some profitable investments. The key is to look ahead and identify potential catalysts that might change the status quo. After all, the only constant in the investment world is change.

Let's start with the North American housing market. It's hard to believe that residential construction has been building such momentum in the last ten years (see chart below). Its success certainly isn't reflected in the shares of its major suppliers: paper, lumber and forestry product companies.

U.S. HOUSING STARTS AND PERMITS, 1967-2003 (fig. 16)

Source: National Association of Home Builders, Bloomberg

The demand for housing has remained strong in the last decade and understandably so. Mortgage rates have tumbled to historically low levels, while a looming economic recovery in North America has bolstered consumer confidence as well as corporate payrolls. This makes it reasonable to expect the market for lumber and building products will continue to strengthen. The steady growth in residential housing construction in 2003 supports this expectation.

As a result, prices for plywood and oriented strand board (OSB is made from compressed wood chips and glue)—both of which are used extensively in residential construction—have been strong for the last few years. It surprises many prospective investors in the forestry sector that the strength of some commodity prices is not reflected in the share prices of the producers. The sector has been grappling with so many negative issues that it is difficult for investors to (pardon the expression) "see the forest for the trees."

Softwood Saga

The biggest issue that has negatively affected the forestry sector is the long-standing and utterly confusing softwood lumber dispute. Journalists have written reams on the subject, while it seems that every politician in the country has taken a whack at cutting it down to size. Delving into this complex trade disagreement in detail would fill the pages of another book, so we're just going to address the highlights here.

Lumber industry lobby groups in the U.S. have been accusing the Canadian government of unfairly subsidizing forest products companies for years. Recently, the U.S. imposed stringent countervailing duties (currently 18.79% at the border), as well as anti-dumping duties (ranging from 6% to over 12%, depending on the company) on all lumber imported from Canada. In the last ten years, Canadian wood has accounted for about 34% of all softwood lumber sold in the U.S.

These duties have severely hurt the ability of Canadian forest products companies to be profitable. For example, Abitibi-Consolidated Inc. pays $20 million in American duties every three months, and wood products represent only 13% of Abitibi's total sales revenues. Other companies affected include Canfor Corp., Weyerhaeuser Co., West Fraser Timber Co. Ltd. and Tembec Inc.

On July 24, 2003 the U.S. and Canadian governments jointly suggested a proposal to their respective lumber industries as a possible solution. Instead of duties, they recommended a cap or quota on Canadian softwood sold in the U.S. market. If a quota arrangement can be agreed to, then the impact on the market would be phenomenal.

A quota agreement would mean that the duties that have already been paid by the forestry companies would then be split evenly between Canadian and U.S. governments. It would take time, but eventually some of these funds would make their way back into company coffers. When that happens, several forest products companies that are currently chronic money-losers would suddenly be turning a profit. It's only a matter of time until this happens.

When the dispute is eventually resolved, the beneficial impact on the industry will surprise research analysts and investors alike, and will act as a catalyst in increasing stock prices.

Paper Chase
A satisfactory conclusion to the heated softwood lumber trade dispute will be a major factor in pulling the sector out of the woods, but other signs show that a turnaround is in the works.

Declining demand in North America and Europe for paper products over the last few years has inspired a great deal of consolidation in the industry. To understand the impact of the mergers, you need to know that there are hundreds of grades of paper and each has its own supply and demand idiosyncrasies.

Let's look at the example of what has happened in the market for uncoated free-sheet (UFS), one of the gazillion paper products on the market today. In 1999, the UFS industry leader, International Paper bought its major competitor, Union Camp Corp. The following year, it acquired Champion, another one of its competitors.

In 2002, Weyerhaeuser acquired Willamette Industries and became number two in the UFS market. Close in third place is the Canadian giant Domtar Inc., which bought E.B. Eddy Forest Products Ltd. in 1998 as well as taking over several mills from its major competitor, Georgia-Pacific, in 2001.

When times are tough, it makes sense for these companies in a mature industry like forestry to increase capacity and streamline their product line. If too many products are stacking up in warehouses at mills that are all losing money, then it's only logical to take the steps to narrow the market—and the easiest means of doing this is to buy your competitors.

Unfortunately, the positive effects of consolidation aren't always immediate. Take the example of the UFS market: at the end of 2003, uncoated free-sheet sold for about $595/ton, which is really close to its cyclical low of $580/ton. But even at this low price, demand still hasn't picked up, leaving the majority of UFS producers awash in red ink.

So is there any good news in the short term? After several years of consolidation in a variety of paper product sub-sectors, the supply/demand balance for most of the forestry commodities looks favorable. Companies are doing a remarkably good job of managing their inventories, which means an increase in demand is the only thing they need to become profitable.

Newsprint Prospects

As you would expect, there's a strong link between consumption and the profitability of paper producers. Increased business activity leads to higher revenues and subsequent profits. Feeling flush, companies then increase their spending on advertising (although many advisors would argue that they should be spending money on advertising in a slow market, but again, that's the subject of another book).

More advertising means fatter newspapers so publishing companies have to buy more newsprint. Large inventories of newsprint are already out there, but these will shrink as paper is consumed. That's when the operating rates of newsprint mills will increase. Once they're operating closer to full capacity, then newsprint prices will start to rise, along with the price of shares in newsprint companies.

NORTH AMERICAN NEWSPRINT PRICE VS. OPERATING RATE (fig. 17)

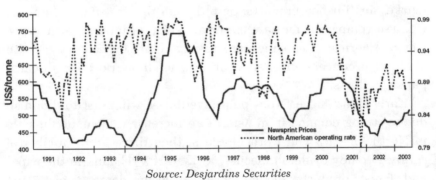

Source: Desjardins Securities

North American newsprint inventories were more than 20% below their five-year average in 2003, thanks to industry consolidation and cutbacks in production. Only recently have newsprint suppliers begun implementing price increases.

An important indicator that better times lie ahead is the ability of forestry product companies to introduce price increases and have their customers agree to pay them. In extremely competitive industries like newsprint, users will only agree to price increases if they need the product. Put it this way—there's no way newspaper publishers would turn down any advertisements just because the cost of newsprint has spiked. They'll pay the higher price and pocket the profits.

Global Rebound

As is the case for all other natural resources, China's rapid economic growth has changed the market dynamics in the forestry sector. China has emerged not just as a major consumer of paper, but also as a producer. Although it's not as blessed as Canada is with a huge natural supply of wood fiber, Chinese companies import significant quantities of pulp, as well as recovered paper (waste paper that is then recycled). Both pulp and recovered paper are used to produce UFS and packing materials such as boxboard and containerboard.

China's increased role as a major producer as well as a consumer of paper is the proverbial double-edged sword for North American paper companies. Exporting raw materials to China is a good business for forest products companies in Canada, Brazil and Russia, but the Chinese are also formidable international competitors in the market for finished products. So although the growing demand by Chinese companies for raw materials such as pulp is good news, North American companies are taking a hit by competing with Chinese producers in a slow international market for finished paper products.

Early signs suggest that pulp inventories will start to diminish due to strong demand from Asia. If an increase in demand for pulp in North America and Europe occurs, then there are a number of catalysts ready to simultaneously kick-start a rebound in the paper and forest products sector. Once European demand picks up, Scandinavian producers won't be so inclined to flood North American markets with excess supplies of their paper products, since their local markets will be able to absorb it all.

Now that the Iraq War and the SARS epidemic are over (and barring any other disasters) a rebound in the North American economy will quickly translate into better pricing for paper products of all types. Credit for the price hike is due to the improved inventory management practiced by a "leaner and meaner" forest products industry. Charles Darwin would be impressed with how this sector has made sure only the strong survived the market purge.

And lastly, the flurry of natural disasters (hurricanes, floods and forest fires) in 2003 was heartbreaking for homeowners but a boon for the beleaguered forestry sector. The unexpected demand for building materials will quickly burn through the current inventory, and subsequently cause the price of raw lumber to increase.

Stock Selection

Once you've decided that it is a good time to invest in the paper and forest products industry, where do you start? When doing your homework, you may find yourself more bullish on some companies and their products than others. No problem. It's possible to manage your portfolio to reflect your gut feelings, at least to some extent.

Canadian companies such as Tembec Inc. and Canfor Corp. (as well as Bowater in the U.S.) are affected by fluctuations in pulp markets more than other forestry products companies. On the other hand, Abitibi-Consolidated Inc. and Norske Skog Canada Ltd. are dependent on a rise in newsprint prices to survive and thrive. West Fraser Timber Co. Ltd. benefits if lumber and plywood prices strengthen, while companies such as Nexfor Inc. and Ainsworth Lumber Co. Ltd. are dependent on the market for oriented strand board.

Don't try to be too ambitious in terms of stock selection. It's difficult enough for experts who have been studying the paper and forest products sector for their entire career to forecast which commodities will move first and which companies will benefit most, never mind the rest of us.

What you can do though is recognize that there are a large number of extraneous factors that can easily throw a wrench into the most comprehensive research and careful analysis, such as:

• *The Money:* Even small currency fluctuations (the U.S. dollar versus the Canadian dollar, and more frequently these days, the U.S. dollar versus the Euro and a host of Asian currencies) can eliminate the profits for some companies. Currency changes basically move the goalposts, making it difficult for companies to figure out the best strategy for scoring. A change in exchange rates can suddenly make it more profitable for a supplier in Taiwan to load bales of paper products onto a barge and ship them to North America. An onslaught in supply from a new source can quickly throw an otherwise stable market into disarray, driving down prices and destroying hopes for a profit.

• *The Mandarins*: In mature commodity industries such as the softwood lumber sector, international trade disputes can develop quickly. Whenever there's any uncertainty in a market, investors get nervous and sell their shares, causing a fallout in the stock prices.

• *The Management*: Who's running the company is an extremely important consideration when choosing companies to invest in. Well-managed businesses, such as Domtar, tend to perform better than others during tough times. The catch is that their shares may not rise as dramatically when the cycle turns and the sector starts to perform well.

• *The Market*: Except for shares in large diversified corporations, many of the stocks in the forestry sector are "thinly" traded, which means the volume of shares bought and sold on an average trading day is much lower than the shares in other large capitalization companies. When they're out-of-favor and analysts are saying the companies aren't expected to perform, it can be difficult to buy or sell the stocks you want at the quoted price. Of course, you will always find a buyer—that's the advantage of the stock market versus other markets—but you have no control over the price you'll get. Always remember that the industry is cyclical, and that trading is more frequent as the sector gets closer to a cycle peak. This is one signal to take your profits and move along. Whenever many people want to buy the stocks you own, sell them.

Chapter Ten
Fertilizers

Diamonds, gold, metals, oil and gas, coal, uranium and forest products are all readily acknowledged as being natural resources. Fertilizers, on the other hand, are rarely considered a natural resource by the average investor even though their roots are similar to other resources. Each resource (with the exception of forestry) originates as prehistoric matter that was transformed by heat and pressure from the earth's core. Now, each is extracted, processed and used for commercial purposes.

Fertilizer is a natural resource that is vital to the growth of the global agricultural industry and is therefore closely tied to trends in that sector. Agriculture is a mature and globally competitive industry—worth more than $95 billion annually in Canada and $1,264.5 billion in the U.S. As a result, it's frequently referred to as "agribusiness" instead of the bucolic term, farming.

Recent scientific advances have opened our eyes to the role that genetics plays in human development though farmers have been practicing this science for centuries. Cross-pollinating plants and breeding livestock to create superior wheat and stronger cattle was an accepted agricultural custom long before genetics became a hotly debated issue.

Likewise, farmers used fertilizers to boost the quantity and quality of their crops long before chemical concoctions were introduced.

While the majority of small farms around the world continue to use livestock manure to enrich their fields, most larger operations rely on less pungent options produced by fertilizer companies.

Resource Links

Fertilizers are to plants like vitamins are for humans: they're nutrients that are needed for living organisms to thrive. The phrase "you are what you eat" is just as applicable for crops as it is for us. Plants need three basic nutrients to be healthy: nitrogen, phosphorus and potassium.

Nitrogen is a fundamental plant nutrient that is found in the air we breathe. Although nitrogen gas comprises roughly 80% of our atmosphere, most plants cannot absorb it in this gaseous form. Instead, they soak up what they need through their roots in the soil. Nitrogen is a key source of amino acids, which simply put, makes plants grow. Nitrogen fertilizers are derived from ammonia.

Ammonia is produced by "cracking" natural gas. (Hang in there, the biology lesson isn't a long one and it is important for investors to understand a bit about this stuff.) The cracking process releases hydrogen which, when combined with nitrogen gas, creates ammonia. The most commonly used nitrogen fertilizer is urea, which boasts a nitrogen content of 46%. What investors should know is that natural gas is a major ingredient in the production of nitrogen fertilizers.

This is an excellent example of how one natural resource subsector is linked to another. Some resources, like natural gas in this case, are essential to the success of other resource-based industries. Frequently one can substitute for another if supply is scarce or if one commodity is cheaper than another at a certain time. What complicates matters for the market is when several industries are simultaneously competing with each other for the same resource.

Other Ingredients

Phosphorus is the de facto "plant energizer" nutrient. A prime source of phosphorous is phosphate, an ore composed of sedimentary deposits on the floors of ancient oceans, driven closer to the surface of the earth by molten lava. The biggest phosphate ore deposits are in Africa, the U.S., China and Russia. As a result, these countries are currently the leading producers of phosphate fertilizers.

Phosphate fertilizer is usually combined with ammonia before it is sold. The two most common phosphate fertilizers are diammonium phosphate (DAP) and monoammonium phosphate (MAP).

Potassium is the third essential ingredient for a number of critical plant processes such as photosynthesis and fruit formation, as well as helping plants resist disease. The word "potash" is derived from an old method of extracting potassium from wood ashes. The majority of the world's known potash reserves are in Canada (45% of global potash production) and Russia (30%).

All right, that's the end of the biology lesson. But even this smattering of facts will give you an advantage over other investors when it comes to buying shares in fertilizer companies.

Feast or Famine

As can be expected, the fortunes of fertilizer companies (as well as farmers) are greatly affected by the feast or famine cycles that are an inherent part of the agricultural industry. Like every other mature sector, when demand is stronger than supply, prices of wheat, grain, soybean or corn rise. Strong prices and revenues give farmers the financial wherewithal, as well as the motivation, to spend more money on products designed to improve the quality and quantity of their crops. Naturally, in boom times there is increased spending on fertilizers and, as a result, higher prices are paid for the commodity.

WHEAT PRICES FROM 1994 TO 2003 (fig. 18)

The last raging bull market in fertilizer stocks began early in 1993 and ended early in 1996. Not surprisingly, the demand for agricultural commodities at that time was especially strong. Grain prices, for example, more than doubled in that time frame (see above chart showing wheat prices over the past ten years).

The primary reason for the spike was a flurry of exports to China. China imported huge quantities of fertilizers, primarily urea and DAP, to support new policy initiatives designed to move the country towards agricultural self-sufficiency. China's leaders had no intention of being held ransom to price hikes in order to feed its enormous population.

But that was then. What's the outlook for the fertilizer industry now? Since the largest increase in agricultural production is in developing countries, and since their economies are robust and show no signs of slowing down, there's a strong case to be made for investing in companies that produce fertilizers.

Ten years after the bull market for fertilizer stocks in the early 1990s, both the global agricultural sector and the worldwide fertilizer industry have changed substantially. China used to consume 20% of the nitrogen fertilizer produced in North America. But by 2000, the Chinese banned urea fertilizer imports, and instead became a leading producer of nitrogen fertilizers. Recent volatility in natural gas prices has put even more pressure on the nitrogen fertilizer industry because they are so dependent on natural gas for the production process.

More bad news for North American phosphate fertilizer producers was in the last few years when countries such as India and Australia entered the market with a vengeance, causing supplies to stockpile in domestic warehouses.

Far East Factor
In the last decade, China has become a major supplier of grain. The country enjoyed bumper harvests in the late 1990s. Since then, it's been consistently exporting its excess grain inventories including corn, in addition to a basket of other agricultural goods such as fruits, vegetables and nuts.

Canada and Australia suffered droughts in 2002, which opened the gates for China and other countries to export into markets traditionally supplied by North American growers. Russia and the Ukraine, for example, filled the gap by plowing their wheat into the global market. Argentina and Brazil joined China in beefing up their exports of corn into massive markets like Africa.

Despite Mother Nature's unpredictable role in the supply and demand of agricultural products, the one thing that we know for sure is that the global population is increasing and people need to be fed. As people in developing countries prosper, an evolution in their dietary demands occurs—they can afford to buy more, and their expectations are higher. Those factors bode well for an increase in demand for agricultural goods.

The catch is that the amount of land devoted to farming is limited and there's no way it can be expanded at the same rate as the population is increasing. The only solution is for the farms to produce more. This is where fertilizers come into play as their only purpose is to improve the quality and quantity of crops.

In 2004, China will continue to be a net exporter of grain to the rest of the world. In spite of this outwardly optimistic sign, and despite the fact that data from China is hard to come by (grain inventories are a state secret), it's widely acknowledged that Chinese grain production has been declining for the past four years. This could mean that China will switch from being an exporter to an importer of key commodities in the next few years. If that proves to be the case, then the market for agricultural goods as well as fertilizer products will grow tremendously.

Fielding Investments
The list of investment prospects in the Canadian fertilizer industry is a short one as only two publicly traded companies are contenders in the global market. Although both companies produce all three types of fertilizers, their product sales mix is different enough so that they are affected by varying factors in the fertilizer market.

Agrium Inc.—founded in 1993 when Cominco Ltd. (now Teck Cominco Ltd.) reorganized its fertilizer operations and acquired the fertilizer operations of the Alberta Energy Company—produces all three types of fertilizers. They also have a substantial retail operation with outlets throughout the U.S. and Argentina.

As with many other natural resource companies, Canadian fertilizer producers often adhere to the motto "go big or go home." Agrium is a good example of this. It's a world leader in the production of nitrogen fertilizers, controlling 3% of the global market and a substantial 20% of the North American market. Because nitrogen fertilizer dominates Agrium's product mix, the company's revenues and profitability are dependent on the demand for this type of fertilizer.

If China's grain inventory is indeed diminishing then that is good news for the corn and wheat markets in the next few years. Growing demand in other developing countries should also create a sunnier outlook for agricultural commodities, as well as fertilizers. The unknown part of the forecast is how dominant China's role will be as a global supplier of nitrogen fertilizer.

Even though the current market for nitrogen fertilizers is cloudy, Agrium has one key factor in its favor. Of all the global producers, this Alberta-based company is literally sitting on the cheapest supply of natural gas in the world. If the price of natural gas declines in the next few years, then Agrium's profits will increase, fueling the company's ability to aggressively compete in the international marketplace.

Diverse Options

With nearly half of the known potash reserves located in Canada, it's not surprising that the Potash Corp. of Saskatchewan is the primary player in the global market for potash fertilizer. Potash Corp. became a publicly traded company in 1989 when the province privatized it. Several years and many acquisitions later, it has diversified its product line so it now produces all three types of fertilizers. Nevertheless, the company's strength still lies in its dominance of the potash fertilizer market.

Potash Corp. also owns the largest, lowest-cost reserve of potash in the world, which gives it the luxury of being the "swing producer" in this market. The company can simply increase or decrease its production depending on how strong or weak the market is for potash fertilizer. Doing so also allows it to virtually control the global price of potash.

For investors who loathe risk, but feel it's prudent to own at least one fertilizer stock as the global economy recovers, then Potash Corp. is an extremely stable option. But don't forget that in a bull market, volatility is your ally. Investors who are more risk-tolerant may choose to own shares in both Potash Corp. and Agrium, while others will skew their portfolios depending on how they feel about the markets. For example, if you're bullish on the agricultural market and bearish about energy, then Agrium will give you more bang for your buck...if you're right about the market trends, that is.

Aggressive investors should take a look at the Canadian upstart Asia Pacific Resources Ltd., which is involved in developing a potash mine in Thailand. China has no known potash reserves and is a massive importer of the potassium-rich fertilizer. The close proximity of the Thai deposit to a massive consumer makes economic sense. The downside, however, is huge—as with all overseas ventures undertaken by junior companies. Protect yourself by examining the political, legal, environmental and economic risks of such a venture before making any decision to invest.

CHAPTER ELEVEN

Flow-Through Shares

"Certainty? In this world, nothing is certain but death and taxes," said American scientist Benjamin Franklin over two hundred years ago. The only difference these days is that while death is still final, taxes can be deferred or reduced.

Canadians didn't always have to worry about taxes. Income tax was introduced as a temporary measure (sounds like the GST saga) to help cover the country's military expenses during World War I. By 1948, the wars were over, but the government decided to not surrender. Instead the *Income War Tax Act* became the *Income Tax Act*.

Since then, Canadians have had to declare income from all sources, including capital gains on the sale of investments or property. We're allowed to deduct some expenses, and there are a few tax credits, but by and large, there aren't too many opportunities for us to reduce our taxable income.

Tax Bite
Taxes are steep and vary greatly depending on where you live. At the time of writing this book, the top marginal tax rates (combining both federal and provincial tax rates) from highest to lowest are: Newfoundland: 48.64%; Quebec: 48.22%; Prince Edward Island: 47.37%; Nova Scotia: 47.34%; New Brunswick: 46.84%; Ontario:

46.41%; Manitoba: 46.40%; Saskatchewan: 44.50%; British Columbia: 43.70%; Yukon: 42.40%; Northwest Territories: 42.05%; Nunavut: 40.50%; and Alberta: 39.00%.

But that's not all. You pay tax on everything you earn as well as on everything you buy. Take the price of gas, for example. In the summer of 2003, it was pumped up to 90 cents a liter in some provinces and more than one-third of the price was taxes: provincial sales tax, GST, and something called the Federal Excise Tax. It hurts even more if you consider that you're paying for the gas taxes with after-tax dollars. Ouch.

One of the best means of minimizing the pain is to take advantage of all the tax deductions that you can. Standard ones include childcare expenses, family support payments, moving and medical costs, and, of course, RRSP contributions.

Unfortunately, not too many taxpayers are familiar with the deductions that are available from investing in the "flow-through" shares of junior Canadian resource companies, or ventures that qualify for the Canadian Exploration Expense (CEE).

You should consult your tax advisor for precise information on the benefits of these deductions for your portfolio, but in the meantime, here's a brief introduction to these tax-deductible investments.

Government Generosity
Buried deep in the *Income Tax Act* (Section 66 (1) to be exact) there's a clause that says: "A principal-business corporation may deduct, in computing its income for a taxation year, the lesser of (a) the total of such of its Canadian exploration and development expenses as were incurred by it before the end of the taxation year..." The Section goes on ad nauseam, but only tax accountants need to get into that level of detail.

What you do need to know from the clause is that most junior energy and mining companies spend all of their money on exploration programs, and usually have little or no revenue. Because they have virtually zero income, they're not able to use all the tax deductions that they're entitled to as a resource exploration company. Mining companies are allowed to deduct prospecting, drilling, geological or geophysical expenses, but if they don't have any revenue, then these deductions remain unclaimed or "wasted."

In a rare moment of generosity, the government decided to allow exploration companies to give up those tax deductions and pass them on to people who can use them. Companies can bundle the tax deductions with their shares then sell them to investors and use the proceeds from the sale of these shares to finance their exploration projects. The ventures don't mind selling off their unused deductions. If they can't afford to keep digging or drilling, they'll be out of business anyway.

These deductions, sold as shares, are called "flow-through shares" because they transfer the tax deductions from the company to the investor. In other words, the government allows a tax deduction that would usually only be granted to an exploration venture to be passed on, or "flow-through," to their investors. It's a win-win situation as the company gets the money to finance their exploration work while investors can claim up to 100% of their investment as a tax deduction.

The government created this program as a means of encouraging people to invest in resource exploration companies. That's nice of them, but given our incredibly high tax rates, it's a good idea to understand how investing in exploration—either in flow-through shares, or in shares of a limited partnership that owns a portfolio of flow-through shares—can help you lower your taxable income.

Limited Partnerships
Investors can buy flow-through shares directly from a company, or own them indirectly by purchasing units in a limited partnership specially created to buy shares in a portfolio of several junior exploration companies.

Buying units in a limited partnership can be beneficial for individual investors because it gives them the tax deduction from the flow-through shares, in addition to reducing their investment risk. A limited partnership can usually buy a much greater variety of flow-through shares than an individual investor could afford to purchase on their own. Therefore, investors in a limited partnership end up owning shares in a basket of startups, rather than just in one venture.

Given that a lot of exploration companies could go bankrupt or walk away from their projects, buying shares in several of them minimizes the risk that you could lose your entire investment.

Tax Credits

How good are flow-through shares as a tax deduction? Are they worth it? The answer varies from one investor to another, but as long as the exploration company—or companies if they're in a portfolio owned by a limited partnership—spends all the money they raised from selling flow-through shares on eligible exploration expenses, then almost the entire amount invested in the shares can be deducted.

A word of caution: don't let the tax appeal of flow-through shares affect your decision-making skills as an investor. Remember that even though the tax deductions alone are beneficial, you're still investing in the riskiest side of the resource industry. It is possible for you to lose all your money if the exploration team repeatedly comes up empty-handed.

On the other hand, investing in an exploration startup by means of flow-through shares does mitigate the risk of losing your investment to some extent. Depending on your marginal tax rate, the after-tax cost of buying the flow-through shares (or portfolio of flow-through shares) is virtually cut in half, compliments of the government.

And there's more good news. In the Economic Statement and Budget Update of October 18, 2000, the Minister of Finance announced a temporary, 15% investment tax credit (applied to eligible exploration expenses) for investors in flow-through shares of mineral exploration companies. Oil and gas exploration companies were excluded.

This announcement introduced a credit, known officially as the Investment Tax Credit for Exploration (ITCE), which reduces an investor's federal income tax for the taxation year during which the investment is made. Although deemed "temporary", the federal government announced in its February 2003 budget that the ITCE is extended by at least one more year.

The ITCE is a non-refundable tax credit that can be carried back three years or carried forward ten years. So if you invest in flow-through shares (of mining exploration companies only) today, you can use the deduction any time up until 2014, or back to 2001. It's a real bonus being able to use this deduction when you need it the most. Keep in mind, however, that the ITCE has to be reported as income in the year after you claimed the tax deductions from the flow-through shares.

The only downside is that when you sell your investment, or trigger a "deemed disposition" (which means the government thinks you've unloaded the investment even if you haven't actually sold it), then you're on the hook for capital gains tax. That's not so bad, as capital gains tax rates are better than regular income tax rates.

Taxing Example

Let's look at how these tax credit programs can help you reduce your taxes. For example, if you live in Ontario and your annual taxable income is $300,000, and you're taxed at the highest marginal tax rate of 46.41%, then you'd pay $139,230 in tax. Of course, to make it simple, we're unrealistically assuming there are no personal exemptions or other allowable deductions and that all income is taxed at the same rate.

If you invested $50,000 in flow-through shares, and the entire amount qualified as a CEE, then 100% of your investment could be deducted from your taxable income. Your taxable income is reduced to $250,000 and you now owe $116,025 in taxes—a savings of $23,205! That's a nice chunk of change that stays in your pocket.

It can get even better. If your investment in flow-through shares is with companies that are exploring for metals and minerals, you'll get an additional tax credit of $7,500. That extra credit would cut your total tax bill down to $108,525. In a perfect world, you could save yourself $30,705 in taxes. Serious money by any standards.

In addition to these federal government programs, there are several provincial flow-through initiatives that we won't address here as they vary tremendously from one province to another.

Real World

Flow-through shares are starting to sound like they're the best discovery since Chuck Fipke dug up some diamonds in the Northwest Territories. As wonderful as they are, keep in mind that since money is made and taxes are paid in the real world, things aren't always as rosy as simplified examples in a book on investing.

Before buying into the example above remember that:

• *Taxes Vary*: Everyone pays taxes on a sliding scale, so not all of your income is taxed at the top marginal rate.

• *Diversify*: Your entire portfolio should never be solely invested in just mineral exploration stocks—diversification is advisable even for investors with an incredibly high tolerance for risk.

• *No Guarantees*: An exploration company is obligated to spend 100% of the money it receives from selling flow-through shares on expenditures that qualify for tax deductions, but if for some reason it doesn't, then you can't claim 100% of the deductions.

The bottom line is that there are many variables that will influence the impact of flow-through shares on your tax situation. Investment advisors can provide details on the limited partnerships or flow-through shares that are available in the market today. Ask them to help you research and screen limited partnership funds so you end up investing in a portfolio of companies that meets your investment objectives.

Investment Goals

Since tax breaks in Canada are few and far between, try to take advantage of any and all legitimate ones. Given that the outlook for some resource sub-sectors is better now than it's been in years —and if you're able to stomach the risk that comes with investing in pure exploration companies—then you could save yourself some money by investing in flow-through shares.

We certainly do not recommend investors throw their hard-earned money straight into assorted ventures just because the companies happen to issue flow-through shares. Not at all. Be sure to use the same careful consideration for evaluating flow-through shares as you would for any other investment.

In conclusion, make sure you:

• Only buy flow-through shares of companies you'd invest in anyway. They should have credible management teams running projects with good prospects. The further along they are in terms of their exploration efforts, the better.

• Don't invest in flow-through shares of companies that are exploring for resources with a bearish short-to-mid term outlook. If it looks like the price of the commodity has peaked, or is about to peak, keep looking. Avoid sectors that are already in favor or overvalued.

• Invest only in limited partnership funds that specialize in sectors that are out-of-favor and therefore undervalued. Even then, make sure you have confidence in the fund manager. It's only reasonable, for example, to expect them to have thoroughly researched the individual securities held in the portfolio.

Lastly, be sure to check with a tax advisor who knows your financial situation before you make any investments, especially in flow-through shares or limited partnerships. Do this before you make the investment, not after, so you can get the most out of Canada's little-known tax deduction.

Chapter Twelve
Evaluating Investment Opportunities

Once you have decided to buy shares in the resource sector, then the hardest part (especially in a boom market) is figuring out which companies are the Real McCoys and which ones are just "promotes" with slick brochures.

The most important factor is to do your own research. The best place to start is by reviewing the Web sites of companies that you're interested in, and perusing their annual reports and press releases. Sure, some of the reports can be extremely dull. Sometimes it seems like they're trying to hide information about what they really do behind a parade of monotonous words.

That's usually not the case. It's more a matter of the companies not doing a good job of communicating with people outside the industry. Take a look at the management teams at most of the junior and intermediate resource companies—they're mostly geologists and engineers specializing in research and exploration and using a vocabulary that doesn't always make sense to those of us who don't spend our summers digging in northern moose pastures or drilling in jungles overseas.

This is why bigger companies (and not just those in the resource sector) have departments that are dedicated to recording, corroborating and translating the research of the exploration team and then presenting it to people inside and outside of the company.

Promoting a company's proprietary and strategic advantages internally to other employees builds morale and instills a sense of pride in the venture. Marketing corporate accomplishments to the general public bolsters the confidence of shareholders, bankers and customers. It's not by accident that the objective of the entire communications process is to ultimately encourage increased spending on research and development.

Necessary Promotion
We're all aware of the lengths that consumer products companies go to in order to convince us to buy their goods. They'll do everything in their power to ensure that a product is readily available when we finally decide to buy.

The same marketing and distribution principles apply to the investment industry. Investment bankers have developed efficient means of identifying worthy businesses that require capital, and to promote them to investors with money and financial ambition. Finance professionals maintain close relationships with large corporations that may require funds for acquisitions or to finance internal growth, but they also scout among the multitudes of established mid-sized companies to find players that look like they could make it to the big leagues if they had sufficient financial backing.

Investment bankers adopt these large and small companies as clients. Then their research departments study the businesses, translating the research into language and concepts that investors can understand. Like their consumer products counterparts, investment bankers try to promote their clients' stocks or bonds as the best investments that will deliver on what they promise. In turn, they make these securities readily available to investors by distributing the research to brokerage branches. Then investment advisors step up to the plate, suggesting to their clients that they might want to buy shares in the companies. Institutional sales desks present the information to more sophisticated investors such as insurance companies or pension plans.

This is the standard process for those companies who are in, or close to, the big leagues. For junior exploration companies, it is extremely challenging to raise enough money to undertake or continue an exploration program, let alone develop a newly discovered ore body into a producing mine. Juniors can't afford to hire the in-house promotional expertise, nor can they access the corporate funds that a senior producer is usually able to. As a small business, they fly under the radar screen of the investment bankers.

Startup Reality
Since it's tough for the majority of small and mid-size resource companies to get financing, then how did mining grow to become such an integral part of Canada's economy? Even the government acknowledges that exploration is fundamental to maintaining our global leadership in mining, and tries to nourish the sector with the generous tax programs discussed in the previous chapter.

The likelihood of investors doling out their savings to a company that "specializes in geologic research and study" are pretty slim. And that's why the sector needs stock promoters. They're to mining what advertising is to cars: it's almost impossible to imagine the product being sold without it. Because junior exploration companies have to compete against hundreds of other similar "products," their promoter has to rely on razzle-dazzle to attract investors. That's how they've earned their reputation as masters of "hype."

"Hype" and "substance" together are a formidable force. Excellent products and ideas won't amount to anything if they don't generate sufficient enthusiasm and support. That's definitely the case in the mining sector.

Sparking the Belief
Without stock promoters, it's unlikely that Canada would have become the global leader in natural resources that it is today. One of the most successful promoters, Robert Friedland, said in 1984 that "if an idea excites the imagination of enough people, the money materializes and the project happens. It happens because there's a consensus of belief. It may take someone like myself to spark the belief, but it's the belief itself that makes it possible."

Most successful mining developments are a combination of geological or engineering talent and determination, and a healthy amount of promotion. It's not enough that the geologists and engineers believe in the project—unless of course, they're wealthy enough to finance their own ventures. Someone has to make investors believe in the project in order to raise enough money to make the company's dreams come true.

Friedland is perhaps best known because of his role as an owner in, and promoter of, Diamond Field Resources, the company that discovered the Voisey's Bay nickel deposit in Labrador. In fact, as the moniker implies, the company was actually looking for diamonds, but in September 1993, two of their freelance geologists Albert Chislett and Chris Verbiski, spotted a rusty outcrop (a telltale sign for a prospector that there's an ore body), while flying along the Labrador coast.

In most cases, if prospectors are hired to hunt for diamonds but they stumble across a rusty anomaly, they would be told to ignore it. Instead, Diamond Field made the unusual decision of sending them back to collect samples. Once it was determined that the outcrop did contain high concentrations of nickel, copper and cobalt, there was ample fuel to fire up their promoters.

Many critics and cynics are eager to denounce promoters every chance they get, but in reality it takes a true opportunist to see a real opportunity. Consider this: Diamond Field shares were selling at $4 in 1994. Two years later, when it was clear that the Voisey's Bay ore body was a massive high-grade deposit, shares sold for $167 (adjusting for an earlier stock split). That's the stuff investment legends are made of.

The sheer size of the deposit made it irresistible to Inco and Falconbridge. Senior resource companies love it when a junior or intermediate company discover and delineate the ore body. If it turns out to be big enough to make it worth their time and effort to develop the deposit, then they usually buy it. In this case, a bidding war erupted between the two senior producers. In January 1996, Inco offered to buy Diamond Field Resources for $3.2 billion. One month later, Falconbridge upped the ante by offering $4.1 billion. In the end, Inco took possession of the junior company for an astounding $4.3 billion.

If it weren't for those two hawk-eyed geologists, and the indefatigable efforts of their promoter, it's unlikely that Voisey's Bay would be on its way to production today. Many investors made a lot of money, and its guesstimated that Friedland personally pocketed roughly $500 million. Though luring, these get-rich-quick stories have a downside.

Stock Fiascos

In June 1995, promoters acquired a small company called Cartaway, which had never been involved in the mining industry. They immediately announced that the company had acquired claims in and around Voisey's Bay. Industry professionals call this sort of promotion "closeology." Whenever a major discovery is made, whether diamonds in Nunavut or gold in Ontario, there's always a flurry of land claims staked around the site. Sometimes mining companies that have solid geological reasons to conduct more exploration in the vicinity stake their claims. But more often than not, news of a discovery also inspires the underbelly of the investment world to get to work too. Greed makes the investing public more gullible and vulnerable to ludicrous claims.

Between April and May 1996, Cartaway issued press releases suggesting that initial test results "confirmed" copper and nickel deposits on their property. In one week, the stock rocketed from $5 to $23. Then the real results were released. The day after the stock hit a high of $23, investors learned there was nothing at all in the Cartaway claim to celebrate. The Alberta Stock Exchange couldn't handle the sudden volume of sale orders and was shut down.

This sort of fiasco should be outlawed, and essentially it is. Securities regulators do their best to protect investors. But just as it is easy to criminalize prostitution, yet difficult to prevent if people are still willing to pay for sex, it's virtually impossible to protect investors who are eager to be shanghaied.

Without a doubt, the most notorious mining scam of all time was Bre-X. Even the beginning of the end of Canada's biggest mining fraud was riddled with irony. On March 10, 1997, David Walsh, president, CEO, and founder of Bre-X Minerals Ltd., and John Felderhof, vice-chairman and the company's top geologist, were to be honored as Canadian Prospectors of the Year at the annual Prospectors & Developers Association Convention.

That same evening, they received a phone call from Freeport-McMoRan Copper & Gold Inc., an American senior producer. Freeport was interested in buying the Busang gold deposit in Indonesia that was Bre-X's claim to fame. As part of its due diligence survey, Freeport had begun its own drilling on the property, and first results revealed insignificant amounts of gold. This was in direct contrast to an earlier report by a third-party engineering company that, based on samples provided by Bre-X, estimated the Busang deposit could contain over seventy million ounces of gold. In one fell swoop, the company's shares, once worth over $6 billion, started to descend into oblivion. They eventually became worthless, except for novelty stores that sold replica share certificates as souvenirs.

Several books chronicle the sequence of events in this incredulous tale of rags-to-riches-to-revelation-to-bust. This scam was the result of what happens when one little white lie grows into several untruths, and if left unchecked, becomes a fraudulent crime. We tell our children to be honest, and read them fairy tales to drive the message home. Well, this is better than a fairy tale for adults, because it really did happen. For all the details, read one of the excellent books on Bre-X. In the meantime, here's an abridged version of the story.

The Bre-X Scam

Bre-X's Busang site had been drilled by previous owners who concluded it was uneconomic. The owners approached Peter Howe, a man who was well-connected in the mining industry, to help them find a buyer for the property. Howe enlisted Felderhof's help to find a buyer. Felderhof was an unemployed geologist living in Jakarta at the time, having worked there as the general manager for a mine that went bankrupt.

Felderhof was a friend of Michael de Guzman, another unemployed geologist. The two men had worked together on one of Howe's projects. In late 1992, Felderhof sent de Guzman to Indonesia to find a deposit that was "worth selling." No doubt anxious to keep working, de Guzman reported back that based on some core samples (which had already been determined by other experts to be of no value) he estimated a resource of twenty million ton of ore was near surface, with more potential and better grades at a greater depth. That was the first lie. The only explanation can be that de Guzman must have hoped the report would keep him employed.

Meanwhile in Alberta, a former stockbroker named David Walsh had been trying, for the most part unsuccessfully, to make a go of it for years in the oil patch. He incorporated Bre-X Minerals Ltd. in February of 1989 and listed the company on the Alberta Stock Exchange.

The unusual name was a blend of his eldest son's first name, Brett, and "X" for exploration. By 1993, Walsh was in dire financial straits. A decade earlier, he'd met Felderhof in Australia and recalled his tales of potential mineral wealth in Indonesia. By this time, many Canadian mining companies were actively exploring around the world, so he made the call. Clearly, his inquiry couldn't have come at a better time for Felderhof and de Guzman. On May 6, 1993, Bre-X announced it had acquired the Busang property for a paltry US$80,000.

Felderhof didn't disclose that the previous drill results on the property were insignificant, and it's likely Walsh wouldn't have wanted to hear about it anyway. Felderhof secured lucrative jobs for himself and de Guzman, as they jointly assumed control of the project.

The first two holes Bre-X drilled were duds. Suddenly, de Guzman proclaimed: "We almost shut down the project...then we made a hit." We now know that the drill cores were crushed (a highly unusual thing to do, but hype quickly displaced any and all concerns about proper procedure) and gold was added to make the grades seem much better than they were.

Salting the Samples

Bre-X had frequently reported the discovery of gold ranging up to 5.68 grams per ton in its drill holes, but when Freeport did their independent drilling in 1997 they found a maximum of 0.06 grams per ton. In industry parlance, the Bre-X samples had been "salted" with gold. The gold that was added wasn't even the right stuff. The ore samples had been mixed with alluvial gold, which is commonly found in riverbeds. Honest prospectors would have seen immediately that the samples were salted because alluvial gold looks significantly different than the type of gold that should've been found in the samples.

Once it was fired up, the promotion machinery just kept gathering steam. Standard industry practice would be to undertake a thorough drilling program, then define the reserves based on rigorous scientific methodology, before even considering potential mine production. Before doing any such drilling, Bre-X management estimated the resource would have an annual production capacity of two million metric tons from a mine and processing plant in Busang that didn't even exist. Blinded by greed, investors and industry experts didn't even question the estimates or query the company's plans.

Bre-X was listed on the Toronto Stock Exchange on April 23, 1996, and then on NASDAQ on August 19,1996. Behind the scenes an ownership dispute was brewing, and instead of disclosing this information, insiders were cashing out their stock options and pocketing millions of dollars. Nevertheless, the stock continued its ascent until it reached an all-time high of $28 in September of 1996, equivalent to $280 before adjusting for a previously ten for one stock split.

In October 1996, the ownership dispute was made public and the stock was battered, reducing the market value of Bre-X by more than $500 million. Things then went from bad to worse. Barrick and Freeport were jostling behind the scenes to wrestle control of Busang, in cahoots with the corrupt Indonesian government.

On February 17, 1997, an agreement was reached. Freeport would buy 15% of Busang, the government would keep 40% indirectly and directly through Indonesian President Suharto's holding company Nusamba, while Bre-X kept 45%. A few months later, all parties discovered they owned a lot of nothing at all.

After the Prospectors & Developers Association Convention, de Guzman disappeared, apparently committing suicide by jumping out of a helicopter. Walsh died of a heart attack in 1998, having moved himself and a few hundred million dollars he'd managed to salvage to a tax haven in the Bahamas. Felderhof and his fortune are believed to be in the Cayman Islands.

In this case, some people made a fortune while others were swindled out of their savings. What about restitution? An Ontario judge ruled that disgruntled Bre-X shareholders cannot sue their brokers, but could launch a class-action lawsuit in Ontario against the company itself. Good luck! Felderhof was accused of violating provincial securities laws, but because these aren't Criminal Code charges, the alleged violations aren't extraditable offences.

Is this how a hoax of such magnitude should end? Probably yes. The little white lie grew to astronomical proportions, but whose fault was it really? It was our fault. Virtually everybody who was a player in the stock market succumbed to the lure of this golden egg. Those who deny ever owning shares in Bre-X probably weren't players in the stock market or they're telling their own little white lie. We were all taken aback when the egg broke and turned out to be rotten inside, but deep down, none of us were really that surprised.

The Real McCoys

Promotion can be used for legitimate and for fraudulent opportunities. But how does an investor learn to distinguish between the Real McCoy and a Bre-X? It's not all that easy for professional money managers at the best of times, but having read this book you are now substantially less likely to be hoodwinked by hype without substance.

The key points to remember are:

• Good promoters are capable of raising money for just about any venture, but they don't always adopt a worthy cause.

• Be suspicious when a promoter attempts to ignite a sense of urgency mixed with greed. "If you don't act now, you'll miss out on making a fortune" doesn't motivate an investor who is interested in out-of-favor industry sectors. Protect yourself by understanding industry trends and knowing company facts.

• Try to do at least some of your own research, so you won't feel like you have to blindly rely upon third-party recommendations and testimonials. Just because others believe in a project, doesn't make it right for you.

• Whenever something seems too good to be true, it probably is.

As you hone your understanding of business and commodity cycles, study the more talented and tenacious industry professionals and track their careers. While fine tuning your stock-picking regimen, you'll begin to recognize the Real McCoys long before they are promoted.

Above all, don't be discouraged by these stories. Windfalls like Voisey's Bay are as remote as the Bre-X debacle. Making money from investing in natural resources is not about striking it rich on a long shot, and most investors don't lose their money because it was invested in a fraudulent company. Successful investing is all about being an educated investor.

Avoid Being a Victim

The tech bubble had more than its fair share of overnight success stories and stings. Even though Bre-X damaged the confidence of investors and made it virtually impossible for scam artists to bilk the public, some unethical characters found a way to still make a quick buck.

In the late 1990s, some dubious junior exploration companies suddenly changed their publicly traded shell companies into "technology incubator" companies, or proclaimed their new business mission was to become a technology company. You can be sure that once resource sectors rebound and begin to receive attention from the press and investment community again, then a whole slew of "former" technology companies will be repackaged as mining exploration ventures.

Just like you wouldn't dream of paying an exorbitant price for a watch from a street vendor who says it's a genuine Rolex, you shouldn't buy stocks in companies that you've never heard of or invest in something you don't know and trust. Above all, never act upon investment advice from a total stranger.

Here's how to avoid becoming a target for unsavory promoters:

• If you come across an unusual company in an industry that you've pegged as one that you're interested in, do your homework or "due diligence" before buying.

• Ask your investment advisor for reports about the company. If the principals have a sordid past, it will likely surface in the information from the research department.

• Search the Internet for a company Web site. Good businesses are proud of their work, are likely to have third-party confirmation of their results done by reputable engineering services companies, and their press releases will usually be more substance than hype.

If anything, Bre-X has made even the most conservative management teams and their board of directors just that much more cautious these days.

• Check the biographies of the company's executives and directors. Biographies should list relevant experience and accomplishments, so be wary if instead of providing details there are bold claims such as "single-handedly discovered" this or that deposit or mine. If there are long stretches of time in their careers unaccounted for, or if they have all of a sudden jumped from a completely different industry, consider that to be a red flag.

• If the Web site is short on content, then look up the company's address or phone number and write or call for current annual reports and press releases.

Boiler-room Set-ups
What should you do if you receive an unsolicited call from a stock-broker or someone claiming to be an investment professional who wants to begin a new relationship by getting you into a sure thing? This does happen, even though it sounds like something out of a movie plot. In fact, there's an episode of *The Sopranos* where a roomful of characters are on the phone pressuring unsuspecting people into buying shares in a company. This is called a "boiler-room" set-up—they turn up the heat until you buy.

In this particular episode, one of the guys makes the mistake of telling a prospect that he recommends they do not buy the shares being promoted. Two thugs eavesdropping on his conversation promptly start to beat him up. When the Mafioso boss sees what's going on he rushes over to pull them off, saying, "Are you guys nuts? Leave him alone. He's the only guy in here with a securities license!"

Unfortunately, boiler-room set-ups do exist, solely for the purpose of separating vulnerable people from their money. They work like this: a bogus company is selected or created, usually with a name that makes it sound like it's engaged in a business that's hot in the stock market, and then insiders start buying the stock on the market to get the price to go up. They call people, tell them to check the stock price, fabricate a story about how there's about to be a signifi-cant discovery if it's a mining play—or a new product, contract or press release if it's a tech stock—that will make the stock go even higher. They pressure people into buying the shares, and just to reel them in completely, they'll keep bidding the stock higher for a while longer.

As more suckers get hooked, the instigators begin selling their shares at the artificially high prices then close up shop. The investors have lost their money and are left hanging on to worthless paper.

How can you avoid this sort of stock market abuse?

• There's nothing wrong with receiving stock tips, but avoid acting upon them without doing your own research. When you receive a tip, your work has only just begun. Check the current state of the industry and leading companies in the sector. Talk to your investment advisor, as there may be a company that's better suited to your investment objectives and tolerance for risk.

• If you're still intrigued by the idea, follow the steps outlined above before buying any shares in the company.

• Even if a stock sounds like a good idea, and seems worthy of further research, there's always plenty of time to buy it. Just because you hear about it from someone, you're not obliged to buy the shares through them. If the person is insistent that you must buy it from them right now, then hang up or walk away. They're a scam artist.

• Many investors like to execute their own trades through discount brokerage services. This is fine if you're in the habit of thoroughly researching the securities you're buying. However, it means you are giving up access to some valuable research that is available to you at no charge if you're working with a seasoned investment advisor at a reputable firm.

Making money from investing in natural resources, or in the stock market in general, is all about research and timing. If you're buying shares in companies in sectors that offer exceptional value because they are misunderstood and out-of-favor (the opposite of hype) then the odds of being stung by promoters and crooks are slim. When stocks you own, or are interested in, start to develop a mass following and begin to attract "hype," you should be selling, not buying.

Finally, prudent investors who are cognizant of how people behave—which really governs how business cycles occur and markets respond—will adopt a balanced approach. A portfolio of senior and junior companies will mitigate risk as well as provide sufficient potential for the occasional windfall.

Greed is the only reason for putting all of your money into one stock or even one sector: if it falls, you lose everything. Just remember, bulls and bears get rich. Pigs get slaughtered.

Chapter Thirteen
Some Key Players

There are thousands of publicly traded companies in the resource sector and it's a daunting prospect for investors—novice or seasoned—to pick and choose which ones to research, let alone invest their hard-earned money in.

So where should you begin? You could start with a sub-sector that grabs your interest, such as diamonds or gold, and then begin to research the high-profile companies in that field. Or you could pick a few companies from each sub-sector and start to do your homework.

The bottom line is that there is no magical means of making sure your portfolio only includes the rising stars and the profitable players in the resource sector. You've just got to start somewhere, do your research, talk to your investment advisor, and make a decision. Once you've made the investment, be sure to continue to keep an eye on the company's activities, watch the commodity pricing, and follow the sector's cycles so you'll know when it's time to sell.

In hopes of making your introduction to Canadian resource companies a little easier, we've lined up a list of fifty prospects listed in alphabetical order by sub-sector. These companies were chosen for a variety of subjective reasons including market position, track record, management team, project location and prospects.

They are an eclectic mixture of aggressive juniors, successful intermediates and stable seniors.

We've included enough details to get you started on learning more about each company. Their Web site address is the best starting point to begin your research.

Diamond Companies
Aber Diamond Corp.

Aber is the only publicly traded diamond producer in the world and they own a 40% stake in the rich Diavik mine.

Resource: Diamonds

Class: Intermediate

Stock Exchange Listings: ABZ on TSX, ABER on NASDAQ

Address:
PO Box 4569, Station A
Toronto, ON, M5W 4T9
416-362-2237
aber@aber.ca, www.aber.ca

Management:
Robert Gannicott, President and CEO
Alice Murphy, VP and CFO

Projects/Locations: Canada (Northwest Territories)

Stock price chart:

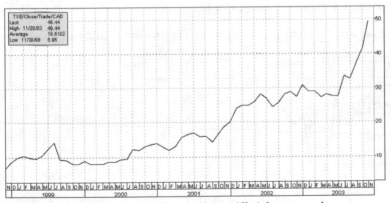

© *Bloomberg L.P. Reprinted with permission. All rights reserved.*
Visit www.Bloomberg.com.

Diamondex Resources Ltd.

The former Winspear Resources management team (they discovered the Snap Lake deposit and sold it to De Beers in 2000 for $480 million) appears to be at it again. Having discovered diamonds at their current projects, they're in a good position to make a second home run.

Resource: Diamonds

Class: Junior

Stock Exchange Listing: DSP on TSX (Venture)

Address:
PO Box 11584
Suite 1410-650 West Georgia St.
Vancouver, B.C., V6B 4N8
604-687-6644
diamonds@diamondex.net, www.diamondex.net

Management:
Randy Turner, President, CEO, Director
John McDonald, Director and Technical Consultant
Caroline Harke, Senior Project Geologist

Projects/Locations: Canada (Northwest Territories, Nunavut, Quebec)

Stock price chart:

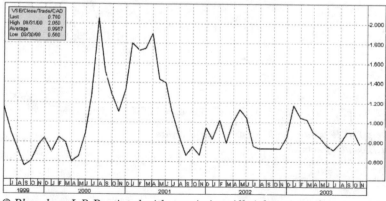

© *Bloomberg L.P. Reprinted with permission. All rights reserved.*
Visit www.Bloomberg.com.

Diamonds North Resources Ltd.

Led by Mark Kolebaba, a former BHP Billiton geologist who was involved in the Ekati exploration and development, Diamonds North has teamed up with Teck Cominco to search for more diamonds in Canada's far north.

Resource: Diamonds

Class: Junior

Stock Exchange Listing: DDN on TSX (Venture)

Address:
Suite 1550-409 Granville St.
Vancouver, B.C., V6C 1T2
604-689-2010
info@diamondsnorthresources.com
www.diamondsnorthresources.com

Management:
Mark Kolebaba, President, Director, CEO
Maynard E. Brown, Director
Bernard Kahlert, VP, Exploration, Director
Yale Simpson, Director

Projects/Locations: Canada (Northwest Territories, Nunavut)

Stock price chart:

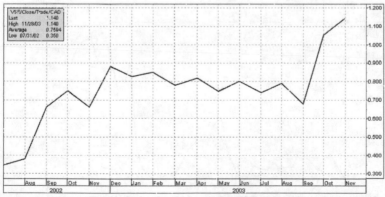

Stornoway Diamond Corp.

Eira Thomas, a former geologist with Aber Resources Ltd. and head of the exploration team that discovered the lucrative Diavik diamond mine in the mid 1990s is behind Stornoway's exploration of eleven million acres in the tundra. Thomas could discover that lightning can strike twice.

Resource: Diamonds

Class: Junior

Stock Exchange Listings: SWY on TSX (Venture)

Address:
Suite 860-625 Howe St.
Vancouver, B.C., V6C 2T6
604-687-7545, 1-888-338-2200 (toll free)
info@stornowaydiamonds.com
www.stornowaydiamonds.com

Management:
Eira Thomas, CEO, President and Director
John Robins, Director, Co-Chairman
Catherine McLeod-Seltzer, Director, Co-Chairman
Bruce McLeod, COO, Director

Projects/Locations: Canada (Northwest Territories, Nunavut, Quebec)

Stock price chart:

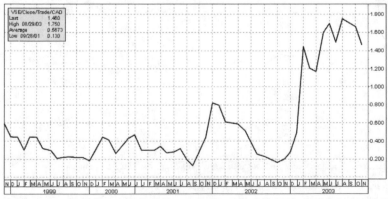

© Bloomberg L.P. Reprinted with permission. All rights reserved.
Visit www.Bloomberg.com.

Gold Companies
Agnico-Eagle Mines Ltd.

This established gold producer with over thirty-five years of precious metals mining experience is sticking to its tried-and-true exploration and development in Quebec's Cadillac Belt.

Resource: Gold

Class: Intermediate

Stock Exchange Listings: AGE on TSX, AEM on NYSE

Address:
145 King St. E., Suite 500
Toronto, ON, M5C 2Y7
416-947-1212, 1-888-822-6714 (toll free)
www.agnico-eagle.com

Management:
Sean Boyd, President and CEO
Ebe Scherkus, Executive VP and COO
David Garofalo, VP, Finance, and CFO

Projects/Locations: Canada (Quebec)

Stock price chart:

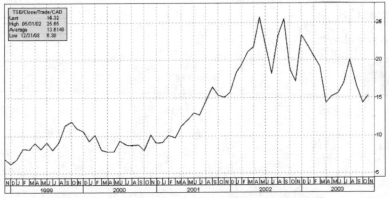

Barrick Gold Corp.

Peter Munk's gamble on a seemingly unprofitable Nevada property in the 1980s vaulted Barrick into the big leagues and they've stayed there ever since. Now they're one of the world's largest gold producers with massive reserves on four continents.

Resource: Gold

Class: Senior

Stock Exchange Listings: ABX on the TSX, ABX on NYSE

Address:
BCE Place, Canada Trust Tower
161 Bay St., Suite 3700, PO Box 212
Toronto, ON, M5J 2S1
1-800-720-7415
investor@barrick.com, www.barrick.com

Management:
Gregory Wilkins, President and CEO
Peter Munk, Chairman
John K. Carrington, Vice Chairman and COO
Jamie C. Sokalsky, Senior VP and CFO

Projects/Locations: Argentina, Australia, Canada, Chile, Peru, Tanzania, U.S.

Stock price chart:

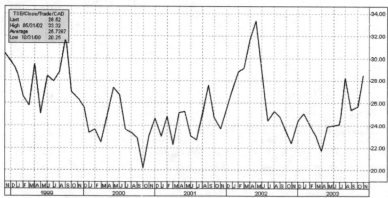

© *Bloomberg L.P. Reprinted with permission. All rights reserved.*
Visit www.Bloomberg.com.

Cambior Inc.

Management has a demonstrated ability to get mines into production at home and abroad. Keep an eye on the results at their Rosebel property in Suriname, the next mine to be added to the Cambior list.

Resource: Gold

Class: Intermediate

Stock Exchange Listings: CBJ on TSX, CBJ on AMEX

Address:
1111 St. Charles St. W., Suite 750, East Tower
Longueuil, QC, J4K 5G4
450-677-0040
www.cambior.com

Management:
Louis P. Gignac, President, CEO, Director
Raynald Vézina, Senior VP
Bryan A. Coates, VP, Finance and CFO

Projects/Locations: Canada (Quebec), Guyana, Suriname, Peru

Stock price chart:

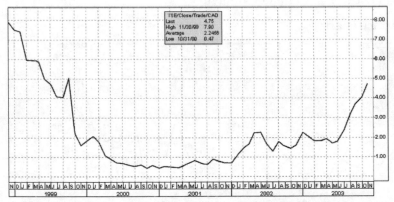

© *Bloomberg L.P. Reprinted with permission. All rights reserved.*
Visit www.Bloomberg.com.

Cumberland Resources Ltd.

Cumberland's Meadowbank Project is on target to become Nunavut's newest major gold mine. Since it's an open-pit mine with the majority of the gold near the surface, they should be well-positioned to finance future projects unearthed by their top-notch exploration and mine development team.

Resource: Gold

Class: Junior

Stock Exchange Listing: CBD on TSX

Address:
Suite 950, 1 Bentall Centre, 505 Burrard St., Box 72
Vancouver, B.C., V7X 1M4
604-608-2557
info@cumberlandresources.com, www.cumberlandresources.com

Management:
Kerry M. Curtis, President and CEO
Brad G. Thiele, VP
Michael L. Carroll, CFO

Projects/Locations: Canada (Nunavut)

Stock price chart:

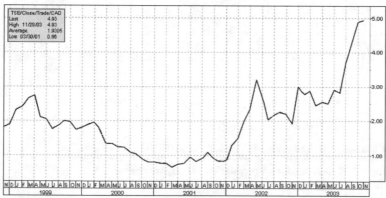

Eldorado Gold Corp.

If their Kisladag project in Turkey works out as expected—production is expected to double and cash costs to decline—then this junior will score big time.

Resource: Gold

Class: Junior

Stock Exchange Listings: ELD on TSX, EGO on AMEX

Address:
920-1055 West Hastings St.
Vancouver, B.C., V6E 2E9
604-687-4018, 1-888-353-8166 (toll free)
info@eldoradogold.com, www.eldoradogold.com

Management:
Paul N. Wright, President and CEO
Earl W. Price, CFO

Projects/Locations: Brazil, Turkey

Stock price chart:

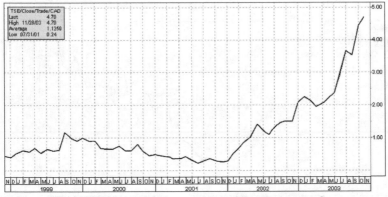

© Bloomberg L.P. Reprinted with permission. All rights reserved.
Visit www.Bloomberg.com.

Glamis Gold Ltd.

In 2003, this spunky junior moved into an intermediate category and has ambitiously set their sights on becoming a serious top producer.

Resource: Gold

Class: Intermediate

Stock Exchange Listings: GLG on TSX, GLG on NYSE

Address:
Suite 310, 5190 Neil Rd.
Reno, Nevada, 89502
775-827-4600
info@glamis.com, www.glamis.com

Management:
C. Kevin McArthur, President, CEO
Charles A. Jeannes, Senior VP, Administration, and Secretary
James S. Voorhees, VP and COO
Cheryl S. Maher, VP, CFO, and Treasurer

Projects/Locations: Guatemala, Honduras, Mexico, U.S.

Stock price chart:

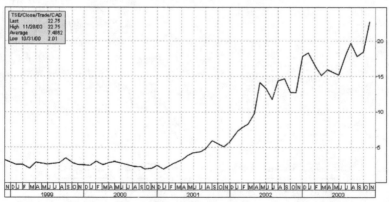

© *Bloomberg L.P. Reprinted with permission. All rights reserved.*
Visit www.Bloomberg.com.

Goldcorp Inc.

Rob McEwen rewrote the rules in the gold industry with the 2001 Goldcorp Challenge. Australians won the prize for their 3D solution to getting gold out of the old mine, but Goldcorp was the real winner with their outstanding results from the low-cost, high-grade Red Lake Mine.

Resource: Gold

Class: Intermediate

Stock Exchange Listings: G on TSX, GG on NYSE

Address:
Suite 2700, 145 King St. W.
Toronto, ON, M5H 1J8
416-865-0326, 1-800-813-1412 (toll free)
info@goldcorp.com, www.goldcorp.com

Management:
Robert R. McEwen, Chairman and CEO
Bruce Humphrey, Senior VP and COO
Brad Boland,VP, Finance

Projects/Locations: Canada (Ontario, Saskatchewan), U.S. (South Dakota)

Stock price chart:

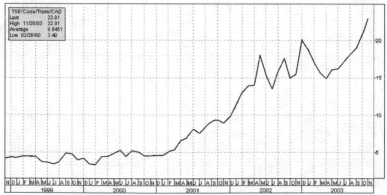

Iamgold Corp.

Diversity is the name of the game for this mid-tier gold producer with overseas operations and a portfolio of properties, including a royalty on the lucrative Diavik Diamond Project in the Northwest Territories.

Resource: Gold

Class: Intermediate

Stock Exchange Listings: IMG on TSX, IAG on AMEX

Address:
220 Bay St., 5th Flr.
Toronto, ON, M5J 2W4
416-360-4710, 1-888-IMG-9999 (toll free: North America)
info@iamgold.com, www.iamgold.com

Management:
William D. Pugliese, Chairman and Director
Joseph F. Conway, President and CEO, Director
Grant A. Edey, VP, Finance and CFO

Projects/Locations: Argentina, Brazil, Ecuador, Ghana, Mali, Senegal, South Africa, West Africa

Stock Price Chart:

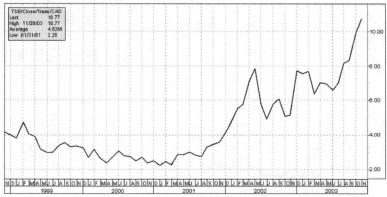

© Bloomberg L.P. Reprinted with permission. All rights reserved.
Visit www.Bloomberg.com.

Kinross Gold Corp.

This gutsy gold producer jumped into a senior category by merging in 2003 with TVX Gold and Echo Bay Mines, proving that it's got the mettle to compete in the big leagues.

Resources: Gold, Silver

Class: Senior

Stock Exchange Listings: K on TSX, KGC on NYSE

Address:
52nd Floor, Scotia Plaza, 40 King St. W.
Toronto, ON, M5H 3Y2
416-365-5123, 1-866-561-3636 (toll free)
info@kinross.com, www.kinross.com

Management:
Robert M. Buchan, President and CEO
Scott A. Caldwell, Executive VP and COO
Brian W. Penny, VP and CFO
John E. Oliver, Independent Chairman

Projects/Locations: Brazil, Canada (Manitoba, Nunavut, Ontario), Chile, Russia, U.S. (Alaska, Nevada, Washington), Zimbabwe

Stock price chart:

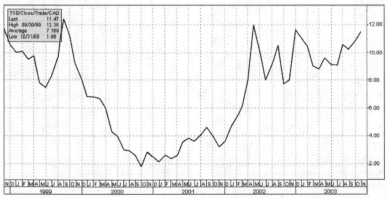

© *Bloomberg L.P. Reprinted with permission. All rights reserved.*
Visit www.Bloomberg.com.

Meridian Gold Inc.

Meridian only has one producing asset, the El Peñón high-grade mine in Chile, but its range of claims in other territories makes this Nevada-based Canadian gold company a shiny prospect.

Resources: Gold, Silver

Class: Intermediate

Stock Exchange Listings: MNG on TSX, MDG on NYSE

Address:
Suite 200, 9670 Gateway Dr.
Reno, Nevada, 89521
775-850-3777, 1-800-557-4699 (toll free)
www.meridiangold.com

Management:
Brian J. Kennedy, President and CEO
Edward H. Colt, Executive VP
Peter C. Dougherty, VP, Finance and CFO

Projects/Locations: Argentina, Canada (Newfoundland), Chile, Mexico, Peru, U.S. (Idaho, Nevada)

Stock price chart:

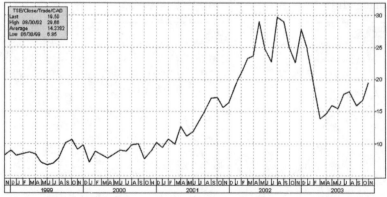

© *Bloomberg L.P. Reprinted with permission. All rights reserved.*
Visit www.Bloomberg.com.

Placer Dome Inc.

An international gold mining company with fifteen mines around the globe, Placer Dome is widely recognized for its world-class exploration and mine development strengths.

Resources: Gold, Copper, Silver

Class: Senior

Stock Exchange Listings: PDG on TSX, PDG on NYSE

Address:
Suite 1600, 1055 Dunsmuir St.
(PO Box 49330, Bentall Station)
Vancouver, B.C., V7X 1P1
604-682-7082, 1-800-565-5815 (toll free: North America, except Alaska and Hawaii)
webmaster@placerdome.com, www.placerdome.com

Management:
Jay K. Taylor, President and CEO
Rex J. McLennan, Executive VP and CFO
Marilyn P.A.Hames, VP, Research and Technology

Projects/Locations: Australia, Canada, Chile, Papua New Guinea, South Africa, Tanzania, U.S.

Stock price chart:

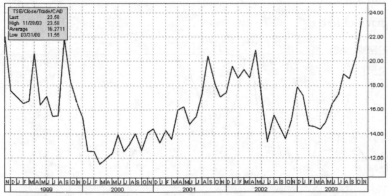

© Bloomberg L.P. Reprinted with permission. All rights reserved.
Visit www.Bloomberg.com.

Base-Metals (Diversified) Companies
Alcan Inc.

The second largest aluminum company in the world with operations in over sixty countries is simply too big to ignore. You name it, they've got it covered in the aluminum market.

Resource: Aluminum

Class: Senior

Stock Exchange Listings: AL on TSX, AL on NYSE

Address:
PO Box 6090
Montreal, QC, H3C 3A7
514-848-8000
investor.relations@alcan.com, www.alcan.com

Management:
Travis Engen, President and CEO
Yves Fortier, Chairman
Geoffrey Merszei, Executive VP and CFO

Projects/Locations: Africa, Australia Austria, Belgium, Brazil, Canada, China, Czech Republic, France, Germany, Hungary, Iceland, India, Ireland, Italy, Kazakhstan, Korea, Malaysia, Netherlands, Norway, Puerto Rico, Slovenia, Spain, Switzerland, Thailand, Turkey, United Kingdom, U.S.

Stock price chart:

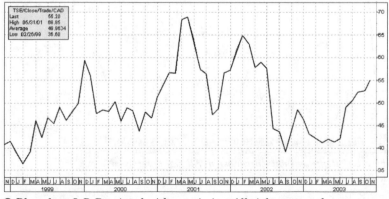

© *Bloomberg L.P. Reprinted with permission. All rights reserved.*
Visit www.Bloomberg.com.

Aur Resources Inc.

Diversified copper producer with successful track records at their operations in Canada and Chile bodes well for their prospects in North and South America.

Resources: Copper, zinc, precious metals

Class: Intermediate

Stock Exchange Listing: AUR on TSX

Address:
Suite 2501, 1 Adelaide St. E.
Toronto, ON, M5C 2V9
416-362-2614
info@aurresources.com, www.aurresources.com

Management:
James W. Gill, President and CEO
Howard R. Stockford, Executive VP and Director
Peter N. McCarter, VP and Secretary
Ronald P. Gagel, VP and CFO

Projects/Locations: Canada (Manitoba, Newfoundland, Ontario, Quebec), Chile, Panama

Stock price chart:

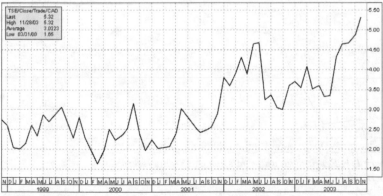

© *Bloomberg L.P. Reprinted with permission. All rights reserved.*
Visit www.Bloomberg.com.

Canico Resource Corp.

Canico acquired the Onça-Puma nickel in Brazil from Inco, so it's just a matter of time before the market will discover if Canico can parlay Inco's interest and former property into a successful producer.

Resource: Nickel laterite

Class: Junior

Stock Exchange Listing: CNI on TSX

Address:
777 Hornby St., Suite 710
Vancouver, B.C., V6Z 1S4
604-669-9446
canico@canico.ca, www.canico.com

Management:
Roman Shklanka, Chairman and Director
Michael Kenyon, President, CEO and Director
Paul B. Sweeney, VP and CFO

Projects/Locations: Brazil

Stock price chart:

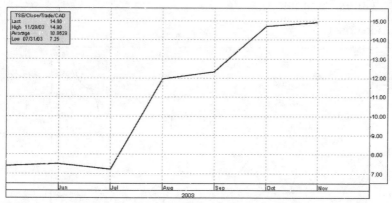

© *Bloomberg L.P. Reprinted with permission. All rights reserved. Visit www.Bloomberg.com.*

Falconbridge Ltd.

A mainstay of Canadian mining, Falconbridge continues to hold its own as one of the biggest and most diversified mining companies in the world.

Resources: Nickel, copper, cobalt, platinum-group metals

Class: Senior

Stock Exchange Listing: FL on TSX

Address:
BCE Place, Suite 200, 181 Bay St.
Toronto, ON, M5J 2T3
416-982-7020
corpcom@falconbridge.com, invest@falconbridge.com
www.falconbridge.com

Management:
David W. Kerr, Chairman
Aaron W. Regent, President and CEO
Michael Doolan, Senior VP and CFO

Projects/Locations: Barbados, Belgium, Brazil, Canada, Chile, Dominican Republic, Japan, New Caledonia, Norway, Russia, South Africa, U.S.

Stock price chart:

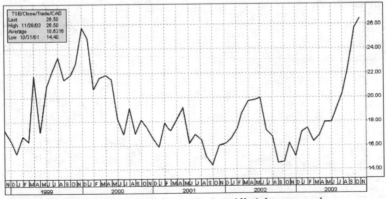

First Quantum Minerals Ltd.

Canadian by listing, the heart and soul of this company is in Africa and it shows. Their local market knowledge and creative engineering abilities has made First Quantum one of the lowest cost producers in the competitive global copper market.

Resources: Copper, cobalt, gold

Class: Intermediate

Stock Exchange Listing: FM on TSX

Address:
Suite 450, 800 West Pender St.
Vancouver, B.C., V6C 2V6
604-688-6577, 1-888-688-6577 (toll free)
info@first-quantum.com, www.first-quantum.com

Management:
Philip K.R. Pascall, Chairman, CEO and Director
Clive Newall, President and Director
Martin R. Rowley, CFO and Director
Michael O. Philpot, Executive VP and Corporate Secretary

Projects/Locations:
Copper Operations: Democratic Republic of Congo, Zambia
Gold Operations: Zimbabwe

Stock price chart:

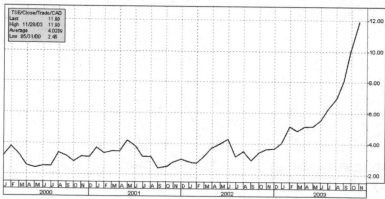

© *Bloomberg L.P. Reprinted with permission. All rights reserved.*
Visit www.Bloomberg.com.

FNX Mining Company Inc.

Hoping they can get an old mine to do some new tricks, the management team of this feisty junior has an option agreement to acquire five Inco properties in the Sudbury Basin—all former nickel/copper operations with great track records.

Resources: Nickel, copper, platinum, palladium, gold

Class: Junior

Stock Exchange Listings: FNX on TSX, FNX on AMEX

Address:
Suite 700, 55 University Ave.
Toronto, ON, M5J 2H7
416-628-5938
info@fnxmining.com, www.fnxmining.com

Management:
Terry MacGibbon, President and CEO
John C. Ross, CFO
Catharine Farrow, Chief Geologist

Projects/Locations: Canada (Ontario)

Stock price chart:

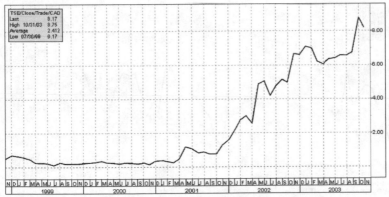

© Bloomberg L.P. Reprinted with permission. All rights reserved.
Visit www.Bloomberg.com.

Inco Ltd.

Inco, the largest producer of nickel in the western world, is on track to increase its share of the lucrative nickel market with its New Caledonia and Voisey's Bay projects.

Resources: Nickel, copper, cobalt, precious and platinum-group metals

Class: Senior

Stock Exchange Listings: N on TSX, N on NYSE

Address:
Suite 1500, 145 King St. W.
Toronto, ON, M5H 4B7
416-361-7511
inco@inco.com, www.inco.com

Management:
Scott M. Hand, Chairman and CEO
Peter C. Jones, President and COO
Farokh S. Hakimi, Executive VP and CFO

Projects/Locations: Australia, Brazil, Canada (Newfoundland and Labrador, Ontario), Indonesia, New Caledonia, Peru, Turkey

Stock price chart:

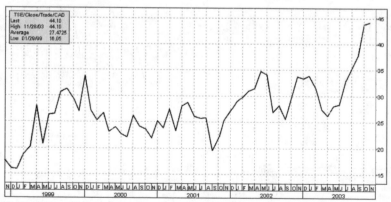

© Bloomberg L.P. Reprinted with permission. All rights reserved.
Visit www.Bloomberg.com.

LionOre Mining International Ltd.

LionOre has taken a major interest in nickel mines overseas, making sure its competitors in Africa and Australia hear it roar as its mines go into production.

Resources: Nickel, gold

Class: Intermediate

Stock Exchange Listing: LIM on TSX

Address:
20 Toronto St., 12th Fl.
Toronto, ON, M5C 2B8
416-777-1985
info@lionore.com, www.lionore.com

Management:
Donald C. Bailey, Chairman
Colin H. Steyn, President and CEO
Theodore C. Mayers, CFO and Corporate Secretary

Projects/Locations: Australia, Botswana

Stock price chart:

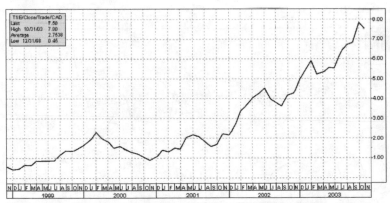

© *Bloomberg L.P. Reprinted with permission. All rights reserved.*
Visit www.Bloomberg.com.

Northgate Exploration Ltd.

Backed by financial behemoth Brascan (it owns 41.6%), Northgate's got the money and the mining savvy to ensure the Kemess Mines become top producers.

Resources: Gold, copper

Class: Intermediate

Stock Exchange Listings: NGX on TSX, NXG on AMEX

Address:
Suite 2050, 1055 West Georgia St.
PO Box 11179, Royal Centre
Vancouver, B.C., V6E 3R5
604-688-4435
ngx@van.brascanam.com, www.northgateexploration.ca

Management:
Terry Lyons, Chairman
Kenneth G. Stowe, President and CEO
Jon A. Douglas, Senior VP and CFO

Projects/Locations: Canada (B.C., Northwest Territories)

Stock price chart:

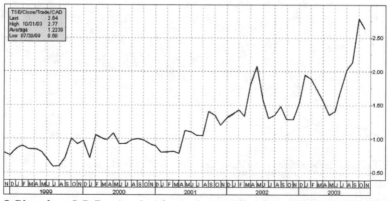

Teck Cominco Ltd.

Varied metals interests and diverse assets as well as a 35% interest in the Fording Coal Partnership gives Teck Cominco a solid base to grow on.

Resources: Zinc, lead, copper, gold and metallurgical coal

Class: Senior

Stock Exchange Listing: TEK on TSX

Address:
600-200 Burrard St.
Vancouver, B.C., V6C 3L9
604-687-1117
info@teckcominco.com, www.teckcominco.com

Management:
Norman B. Keevil, Chairman
David A. Thompson, Deputy Chairman and CEO
John G. Taylor, Senior VP, Finance and CFO
John F.H. Thompson, Chief Geoscientist

Projects/Locations: Brazil, Australia, Canada, Chile, Mexico, Namibia, Peru, Turkey, U.S.

Stock price chart:

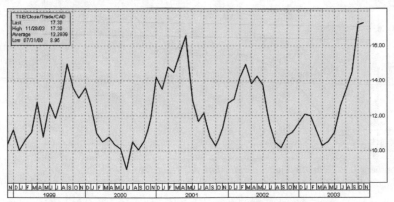

© *Bloomberg L.P. Reprinted with permission. All rights reserved.*
Visit www.Bloomberg.com.

Wolfden Resources Inc.

Ewan Downie has launched a number of promising exploration projects supported by a balance sheet with no debt and a backup of $32 million in cash.

Resources: Gold and base metals

Class: Junior

Stock Exchange Listing: WLF on TSX

Address:
56 Temperance St., 4th Fl.
Toronto, ON, M5H 3V5
1-807-473-6723 (toll free)
wolfden@baynet.net, www.wolfdenresources.com

Management:
Ewan S. Downie, President and CEO
Henry J. Knowles, Chairman
John Seaman, CFO

Projects/Locations: Canada (Manitoba, Nunavut, Ontario, Quebec)

Stock price chart:

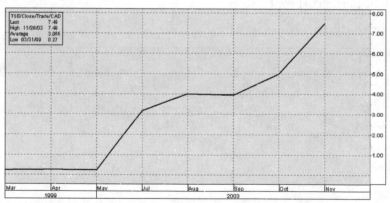

Energy Companies
Atlas Energy Ltd.

They don't seem like they're carrying the weight of the world on their shoulders with their energetic exploration and development activity in southern Alberta.

Resources: Natural gas, crude oil

Class: Junior

Stock Exchange Listing: AED on TSX

Address:
Suite 800, 407 2nd St. S.W.
Calgary, AB, T2P 2Y3
403-215-8313
info@atlasenergyltd.com, www.atlasenergyltd.com

Management:
Lloyd C. Swift, President
Richard Lewanski, President and CEO
James C. Lough, VP, CFO

Projects/Location: Canada (Alberta)

Stock price chart:

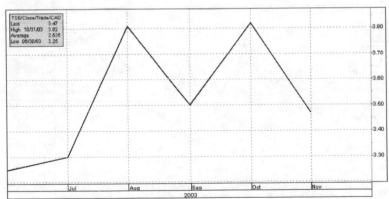

Canadian Natural Resources Ltd.

CNR has moved from a start-up position to a major player and ensured its position as one of the most successful growth companies in the Canadian oil patch.

Resources: Oil, natural gas

Class: Senior

Stock Exchange Listings: CNQ on TSX, CNQ on NYSE

Address:
Suite 2500, 855 2nd St. S.W.
Calgary, AB, T2P 4J8
403-517-6700
www.cnrl.com

Management:
Allan P. Markin, Chairman
John G. Langille, President
Steve W. Laut, COO
Douglas A. Proll, Senior VP, Finance

Projects/Locations: Canada, North Sea, offshore West Africa

Stock price chart:

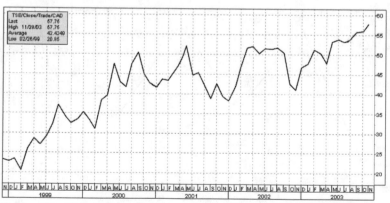

© *Bloomberg L.P. Reprinted with permission. All rights reserved.*
Visit www.Bloomberg.com.

EnCana Corp.

Formed in 2002 through the merger of Alberta Energy Company Ltd. and PanCanadian Energy Corp., EnCana is now the largest independent North American natural gas producer with a dominant position at home and a growing presence overseas.

Resources: Oil, gas

Class: Senior

Stock Exchange Listings: ECA on TSX, ECA on NYSE

Address:
150-9th Ave. S.W.
PO Box 2850, Calgary, AB, T2P 2S5
403-645-3550
investor.relations@encana.com, www.encana.com

Management:
Gwyn Morgan, President and CEO
Randy Eresman, Executive VP and COO
John Watson, Executive VP and CFO
Roger Biemans, President EnCana Oil and Gas (U.S.) Inc.

Projects/Locations: Barbados, Brazil, Canada, Chad, Ecuador, Qatar, United Arab Emirates, United Kingdom, U.S., Yemen

Stock price chart:

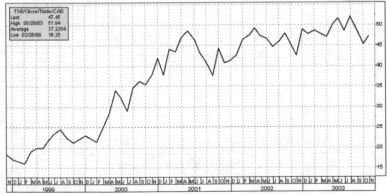

© Bloomberg L.P. Reprinted with permission. All rights reserved.
Visit www.Bloomberg.com.

Husky Energy Inc.

Since it was listed in August 2000, Husky has proven that—aside from its mascot—it's no dog. Acquisitions and a diverse range of operations will have it nipping at the heels of its competitors for years to come.

Resources: Oil, gas

Class: Senior

Stock Exchange Listing: HSE on TSX

Address:
707-8th Ave. S.W.
Box 6525, Station "D"
Calgary, AB, T2P 3G7
403-298-6111
webmaster@huskyenergy.ca, www.huskyenergy.com

Management:
John C.S. Lau, President and CEO
Neil D. McGee, VP and CFO

Projects/Locations: Canada, China

Stock price chart:

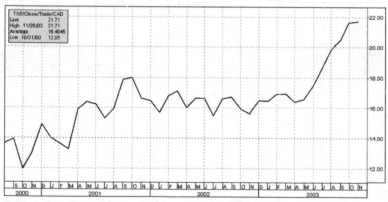

© *Bloomberg L.P. Reprinted with permission. All rights reserved. Visit www.Bloomberg.com.*

Ketch Resources Ltd.

Its predecessor, Ketch Energy, was a short-lived success story before it merged with Acclaim Energy Trust in 2002. Ketch Resources was created to renew an exploration program on the lands of its former entity and has met with great drilling success.

Resources: Natural gas, crude oil

Class: Junior

Stock Exchange Listing: KER on TSX

Address:
Suite 1100, 530 8th Ave. S.W.
Calgary, AB, T2P 3S8
403-213-3100
info@ketchresources.com, www.ketchresources.com

Management:
Grant Fagerheim, President and CEO
Darryl Metcalfe, VP, Exploration and Development
Steve Nikiforuk, VP, Finance and Controller
Tony Smith, VP, Land
Kirby Wanner, VP, Engineering and Operations

Projects/Locations: Canada (Alberta)

Stock price chart:

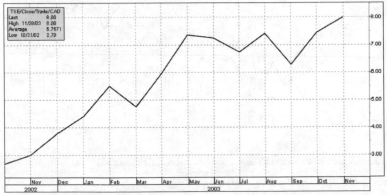

© *Bloomberg L.P. Reprinted with permission. All rights reserved.*
Visit www.Bloomberg.com.

Petro-Canada Ltd.

They've succeeded in putting the maple leaf on oil and gas production and refineries across the country and around the world. With such diverse operations, it's worth flagging Petro-Canada.

Resources: Oil, gas

Class: Senior

Stock Exchange Listings: PCA on TSX, PCZ on NYSE

Address:
PO Box 2844
Calgary, AB, T2P 3E3
403-296-8000
investor@petro-canada.ca, www.petro-canada.ca

Management:
Ron A. Brenneman, CEO
Norman I. McIntyre, President
Harry Roberts, Senior VP and CFO

Projects/Locations: Algeria, Canada, Denmark, Faroe Islands, Germany, Kazakhstan, Libya, Netherlands, Syria, Trinidad and Tobago, Tunisia, United Kingdom, U.S., Venezuela

Stock price chart:

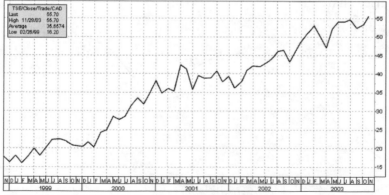

© *Bloomberg L.P. Reprinted with permission. All rights reserved.*
Visit www.Bloomberg.com.

Progress Energy Ltd.

The management team that made Encal Energy such an excellent company left to launch Progress after Encal was acquired by an American company. Odds are they're going to duplicate their past success.

Resources: Crude oil, natural gas

Class: Junior

Stock Exchange Listing: PGX on TSX

Address:
Suite 1400, 440 2nd Ave. S.W.
Calgary, AB, T2P 3R7
403-216-2510
ir@progressenergy.com, www.progressenergy.com

Management:
John M. Stewart, Chairman
David D. Johnson, President and CEO
Steven A. Allaire, VP, Finance and CFO, and Secretary

Project/Locations: Canada (Alberta, B.C.)

Stock price chart:

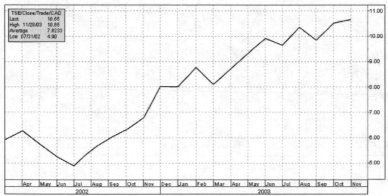

Suncor Energy Inc.

They've got energy to burn: producing and selling oil and gas, operating a refinery, and marketing refined petroleum products.

Resources: Crude oil, natural gas

Class: Senior

Stock Exchange Listings: SU on TSX, SU on NYSE

Address:
PO Box 38, 112-4th Ave. S.W.
Calgary, AB, T2P 2V5
403-269-8100, 1-866-786-2671 (toll free)
info@suncor.com, www.suncor.com

Management:
Rick George, President, CEO
Kenneth Alley, Senior VP and CFO

Projects/Locations: Canada (Alberta, Ontario), U.S. (Colorado, Wyoming)

Stock price chart:

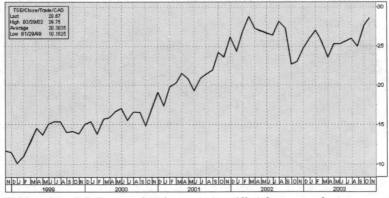

© *Bloomberg L.P. Reprinted with permission. All rights reserved.*
Visit www.Bloomberg.com.

Talisman Energy Inc.

A powerhouse in the energy sector, Talisman is an international exploration and production company with a diversified asset base.

Resources: Oil, natural gas

Class: Senior

Stock Exchange Listings: TLM on TSX, TLM on NYSE

Address:
Suite 3400, 888-3rd St. S.W.
Calgary, AB, T2P 5C5
403-237-1234
tlm@talisman-energy.com, www.talisman-energy.com

Management:
Douglas D. Baldwin, Chairman
James W. Buckee, President and CEO
Michael D. McDonald, Executive VP, Finance and CFO
Ron J. Eckhardt, Executive VP, North American Operations

Projects/Locations: Algeria, Canada, Colombia, Indonesia, Malaysia, Norway, Qatar, Sudan, Trinidad, United Kingdom, U.S., Vietnam

Stock price chart:

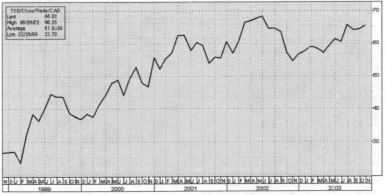

Tempest Energy Corp.

In the crowded Albertan oil patch where oil rigs seem to be everywhere, this company has carved out access to large blocks of undeveloped land.

Resources: Oil, gas

Class: Junior

Stock Exchange Listing: TMY on TSX

Address:
Suite 2800, 500-4th Ave. S.W.
Calgary, AB, T2P 2V6
403-262-2936
www.tempestenergy.com

Management:
A. Scott Dawson, President, CEO, Director
Douglas N. Penner, VP, Finance and CFO
Gerald R. Costigan, VP, Explorations

Projects/Locations: Canada (Alberta)

Stock price chart:

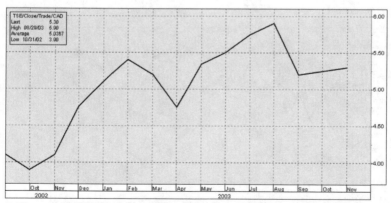

Uranium Companies
Cameco Corp.

The world's largest publicly traded uranium company and a significant gold producer diversified its operations by acquiring 31.6% of Bruce Power in Canada.

Resources: Uranium, gold

Class: Senior

Stock Exchange Listings: CCO on TSX, CCJ on NYSE

Address:
2121 11th St. W.
Saskatoon, SK, S7M 1J3
306-956-6200
www.cameco.com

Management:
Gerald W. Grandey, President and CEO
Terry V. Rogers, Senior VP and COO
George B. Assie, Senior VP, Marketing and Business Development
David M. Petroff, Senior VP, Finance and Administration, and CFO

Projects/Locations: Canada (Ontario, Saskatchewan), Kyrgyzstan, Mongolia, U.S. (Nebraska, Wyoming)

Stock price chart:

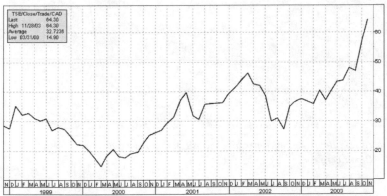

UEX Corp.

UEX has acquired interests in several properties in Saskatchewan, a region that accounts for more than 30% of the global uranium production. Cameco owns 35.3% of this aggressive explorer.

Resource: Uranium

Class: Junior

Stock Exchange Listing: UEX-T on TSX

Address:
Suite 1007, 808 Nelson St.
Box 12151, Nelson Square
Vancouver, B.C., V6Z 2H2
604-669-2349
info@uex-corporation.com, www.uex-corporation.com

Management:
Stephen Sorensen, President, CEO and Director
Warren Stanyer, Corporate Secretary

Projects/Locations: Canada (Saskatchewan)

Stock price chart:

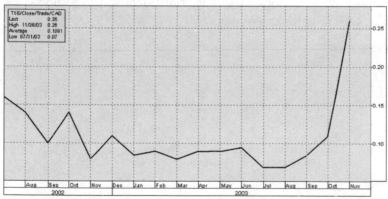

© *Bloomberg L.P. Reprinted with permission. All rights reserved.*
Visit www.Bloomberg.com.

Coal Companies
Fording Canadian Coal Trust

The world's largest producer of the industrial mineral wollastonite (typically found in limestone; a silicate of calcium, used as a filler in plastics, paints, resins and ceramics) and the second largest exporter of metallurgical coal makes this partnership an interesting prospect.

Resources: Coal, wollastonite

Class: Senior

Stock Exchange Listings: FDG.UN on TSX, FDG on NYSE

Address:
Suite 1000, 205-9th Ave. S.E.
Calgary, AB, T2G 0R4
403-260-9800
investors@fording.ca, www.fording.ca

Management:
Michael A. Grandin, Chairman and CEO
Jim G. Gardiner, President
Jim L. Popowich, Executive VP
Ron A. Millos, CFO

Projects/Locations: Canada (Alberta, B.C.)

Stock price chart:

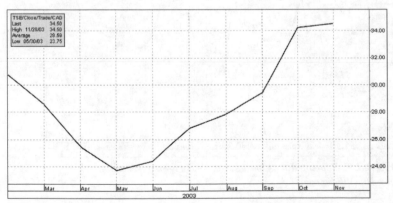

Sherritt International Corp.

One of the most diversified companies in the resources sector, Sherritt stands to benefit from its ownership of energy, metals and fertilizer operations as well as tourism, telecommunications and food processing companies.

Resources: Coal, nickel, oil and gas, fertilizer

Class: Senior

Stock Exchange Listing: S on TSX

Address:
1133 Yonge St., 5th Fl.
Toronto, ON, M4T 2Y7
416-924-4551, 1-800-704-6698
www.sherritt.com

Management:
Ian W. Delaney, Chairman
Dennis G. Maschmeyer, President and CEO

Projects/Locations: Canada (Alberta, Ontario), Cuba, Netherlands, Spain

Stock price chart:

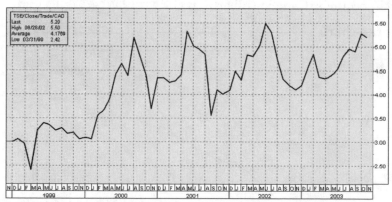

© *Bloomberg L.P. Reprinted with permission. All rights reserved.*
Visit www.Bloomberg.com.

Fertilizer Companies
Agrium Inc.

Acquiring Unocal Corp.'s fertilizer assets made Agrium one of the top two nitrogen producers in the world. Operating more than two hundred and twenty-five retail farm centers in the U.S. ensures their product will continue to do well in the field.

Resources: Nitrogen, phosphate, potash, sulphur

Class: Senior

Stock Exchange Listings: AGU on TSX, AGU on NYSE

Address:
13131 Lake Fraser Dr. S.E.
Calgary, AB, T2J 7E8
403-225-7000, 1-877-247-4861 (toll free)
investor@agrium.com, www.agrium.com

Management:
Michael M. Wilson, President and CEO
Bruce G. Waterman, Senior VP, Finance and CFO

Projects/Locations: Argentina, Canada, U.S.

Stock price chart:

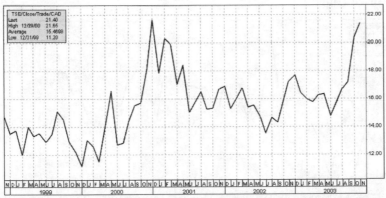

© Bloomberg L.P. Reprinted with permission. All rights reserved.
Visit www.Bloomberg.com.

Potash Corp. of Saskatchewan

The world's largest fertilizer company controls almost two-thirds of global excess potash capacity, has a strong strategic position in phosphates, and is one of the world's largest nitrogen producers. Watch them grow.

Resources: Nitrogen, phosphate, potash

Class: Senior

Stock Exchange Listings: POT on TSX, POT on NYSE

Address:
Suite 500, 122 1st Ave. S.
Saskatoon, SK, S7K 7G3
306-933-8500, 1-800-667-0403 (within Canada)
1-800-667-3930 (U.S.)
pr@potashcorp.com, www.potashcorp.com

Management:
William J. Doyle, President and CEO
James F. Dietz, Executive VP and COO
Wayne R. Brownlee, Senior VP, Treasurer and CFO

Projects/Locations: Brazil, Canada, Chile, Trinidad, U.S.

Stock price chart:

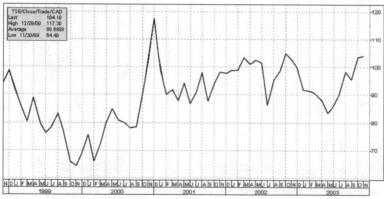

© *Bloomberg L.P. Reprinted with permission. All rights reserved.*
Visit www.Bloomberg.com.

Paper and Forestry Companies
Abitibi-Consolidated Inc.

The world's largest newsprint and uncoated groundwood paper manufacturer is the most widely held stock of all the Canadian paper and forestry products companies.

Resources: Newsprint, uncoated groundwood paper

Class: Senior

Stock Exchange Listings: A on TSX, ABY on NYSE

Address:
Suite 800, 1155 Metcalfe St.
Montreal, QC, H3B 5H2
514-875-2160
info@abitibiconsolidated.com, www.abitibiconsolidated.com

Management:
John W. Weaver, President, CEO
Richard Drouin, Chairman
Pierre Rougeau, Senior VP, Corporate Development and CFO

Projects/Locations: Canada (Ontario, Quebec), China, South Korea, Thailand, United Kingdom, U.S.

Stock price chart:

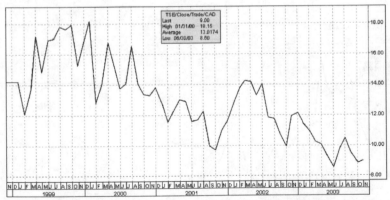

© *Bloomberg L.P. Reprinted with permission. All rights reserved.*
Visit www.Bloomberg.com.

Canfor Corp. (Canadian Forest Products)

The largest lumber and kraft market pulp producer in the country and the fourth largest Canadian paper and forestry products company managed to stand tall and not be toppled by the downturns in the forestry sector.

Resource: Softwood lumber

Class: Senior

Stock Exchange Listing: CFP on TSX

Address:
Bentall 5
Suite 1500, 550 Burrard St.
Vancouver, B.C., V6C 2C1
604-661-5241
invest@canfor.ca, www.canfor.ca

Management:
David L. Emerson, President and CEO
Peter J.G. Bentley, Chairman
Charles W. Reid, Group VP, Finance, CFO
Barbara R. Hislop, Group VP, Chief Technology Officer

Projects/Locations: Canada (Alberta, B.C., Quebec), U.S. (Washington State)

Stock price chart:

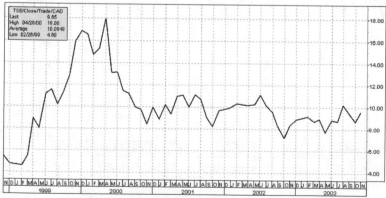

© *Bloomberg L.P. Reprinted with permission. All rights reserved.*
Visit www.Bloomberg.com.

Cascades Inc.

A major producer of various paper products, Cascades is consistently profitable because of the less cyclical nature of its product line. It prospers in a slow market because the cost of waste paper, its primary raw material, plummets during a down cycle.

Resources: Packaging and boxboard products, fine papers, tissue papers, hygienic and specialty products.

Class: Senior

Stock Exchange Listing: CAS on TSX

Address:
404 Marie-Victorin Blvd., PO Box 30
Kingsey Falls, QC, J0A 1B0
819-363-5100
info@cascades.com, www.cascades.com

Management:
Bernard Lemaire, Chairman
Alain Lemaire, President and CEO
Laurent Lemaire, Executive Vice-Chairman
Andre Belzile, VP, CFO

Projects/Locations: Canada, England, France, Germany, Mexico, Sweden, U.S.

Stock price chart:

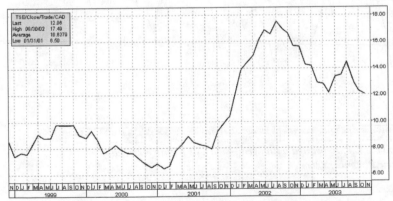

© *Bloomberg L.P. Reprinted with permission. All rights reserved.*
Visit www.Bloomberg.com.

Domtar Inc.

Diversified operations is one reason why North America's third largest uncoated free-sheet producer and one of the continent's major distributors of paper and graphic arts supplies has reported some real paper profits.

Resources: Uncoated paper, lumber, wood products

Class: Senior

Stock Exchange Listings: DTC on TSX, DTC on NYSE

Address:
395 de Maisonneuve Blvd. W.
Montreal, QC, H3A 1L6
514-848-5400
www.domtar.com

Management:
Jacques Girard, Chairman
Raymond Royer, President and CEO
Christian Dubé, Senior VP and CFO

Projects/Locations: Canada, France, Mexico, U.S.

Stock price chart:

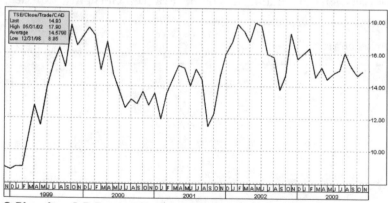

© *Bloomberg L.P. Reprinted with permission. All rights reserved.*
Visit www.Bloomberg.com.

Nexfor Inc.

Diversified producer of specialty papers, pulp and building materials, they're also the United Kingdom's largest producer of wood-based panels.

Resources: Panels, paper, timber, lumber

Class: Intermediate

Stock Exchange Listing: NF on TSX

Address:
Suite 500, 1 Toronto St.
Toronto, ON, M5C 2W4
416-643-8820, 1-877-2NEXFOR (toll free)
www.nexfor.com

Management:
Dominic Gammiero, President and CEO
John Tremayne, Executive VP, Finance and CFO
Bert Martin, Executive VP, Paper
J. Barrie Shineton, Executive VP, Wood Products

Projects/Locations: Canada, United Kingdom, U.S.

Stock price chart:

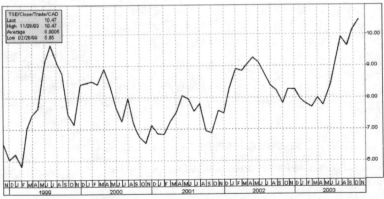

© Bloomberg L.P. Reprinted with permission. All rights reserved.
Visit www.Bloomberg.com.

Riverside Forest Products Ltd.

Canada's largest producer of softwood plywood and veneer, and a major manufacturer of stud and random length lumber has branched out into producing a large range of value-added products.

Resources: Softwood plywood, veneer and lumber

Class: Intermediate

Stock Exchange Listing: RFP on TSX

Address:
820 Guy St.
Kelowna, B.C., V1Y 7R5
250-762-3411
info@riverside.bc.ca, www.riverside.bc.ca

Management:
Gordon Steele, Chairman, President, CEO
Michael Moore, CFO

Projects/Locations: Canada (B.C.)

Stock price chart:

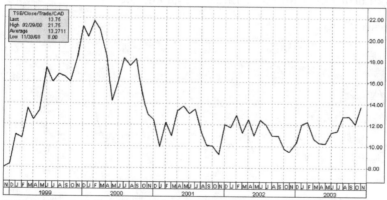

© *Bloomberg L.P. Reprinted with permission. All rights reserved.*
Visit www.Bloomberg.com.

Tembec Inc.

A fully integrated pulp, newsprint and wood products company, Tembec is Canada's largest seller of market pulp.

Resources: Wood products, market pulp, paper

Class: Senior

Stock Exchange Listing: TBC on TSX

Address:
Suite 1050, 800 René-Lévesque Blvd. W.
Montreal, QC, H3B 1X9
514-871-0137
www.tembec.ca

Management:
Claude Boivin, Director
Frank A. Dottori, President and CEO
Michel Dumas, Executive VP, Finance and CFO
Charles Gagnon, VP, Corporate Relations

Projects/Locations: Canada, Chile, France, U.S.

Stock price chart:

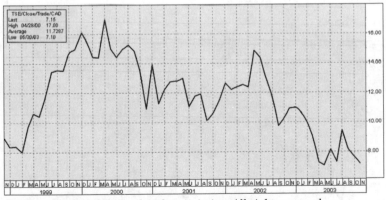

TimberWest Forest Corp.

The largest owner of private timberlands in western Canada has built on its local customer base to become a major exporter of logs to the Japanese and U.S. markets.

Resource: Timber

Class: Intermediate

Stock Exchange Listing: TWF.UN on TSX

Address:
Suite 2300, 1055 West Georgia St.
PO Box 11101
Vancouver, B.C., V6E 3P3
604-654-4600
Bev_Park@timberwest.com, www.timberwest.com

Management:
V. Edward Daughney, Chairman
Paul J. McElligott, President and CEO
Beverlee Park, VP, Finance and CFO
Hamish Kerr, VP, Strategic Planning and Forest Policy

Projects/Locations: Canada (B.C.)

Stock price chart:

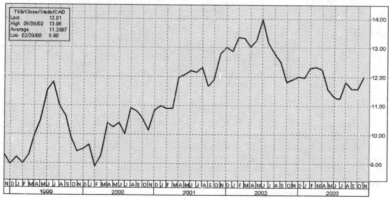

© *Bloomberg L.P. Reprinted with permission. All rights reserved.*
Visit www.Bloomberg.com.

Beyond 2004: Can the boom last?

Timing is everything—in love, in life, and undeniably, in investments. The "Investing in Resources" graph on the next page is a tongue-in-cheek look at the way most people time their purchases and sales of shares in the resource sector. It's human nature to get caught up in the momentum of the market, and despite painful lessons, many investors repeat the same mistakes: they buy when the market is hot, and sell when it's in a slump.

The only way to profit from the boom-and-bust cycles in the resource sector is to pay close attention to the timing of your investments. Be ready for the boom to begin, take a shotgun approach and diversify your holdings, then watch the market closely for signs that it's a good time to sell.

The title of this book implies that the resources market as a whole is ready to boom. It's important to remember that while resources are indeed one sector, each commodity moves to the beat of its own cycle. At any one point in time, some sub-sectors will be taking off, others may have already peaked, while a few are bound to be engaged in a downward spiral. Some are linked, such as natural gas and fertilizer industries, but the majority of the sub-sectors operate independently of each other. Therefore, the odds of them all booming at the same time are extremely slim.

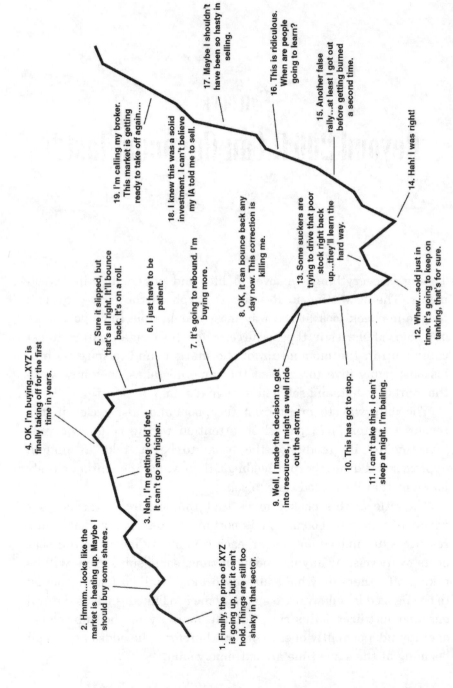

1. Finally, the price of XYZ is going up, but it can't hold. Things are still too shaky in that sector.

2. Hmmm...looks like the market is heating up. Maybe I should buy some shares.

3. Nah, I'm getting cold feet. It can't go any higher.

4. OK, I'm buying...XYZ is finally taking off for the first time in years.

5. Sure it slipped, but that's all right. It'll bounce back. It's on a roll.

6. I just have to be patient.

7. It's going to rebound. I'm buying more.

8. OK, it can bounce back any day now. This correction is killing me.

9. Well, I made the decision to get into resources, I might as well ride out the storm.

10. This has got to stop.

11. I can't take this. I can't sleep at night. I'm bailing.

12. Whew...sold just in time. It's going to keep on tanking, that's for sure.

13. Some suckers are trying to drive that poor stock right back up...they'll learn the hard way.

14. Hah! I was right!

15. Another false rally...at least I got out before getting burned a second time.

16. This is ridiculous. When are people going to learn?

17. Maybe I shouldn't have been so hasty in selling.

18. I knew this was a solid investment. I can't believe my IA told me to sell.

19. I'm calling my broker. This market is getting ready to take off again....

The next question that most people want to ask about timing is how long will the boom in natural resources last. Well, that depends on a variety of factors over which no one has any control. If the global economy picks up steam as expected, then the rally could conceivably go on for years. But setbacks can occur—either economic or, worst of all, war or terrorist attacks—that can derail the boom at any time. Since there is no pat answer as to how long it can last, the secret to profiting from investing in resources is to watch the signs and make your moves. Forget the old investment mantra of "buy and hold." The maxim for this sector is "buy and watch."

Selling a winning stock is arguably much more difficult than buying a good prospect. But it's far more critical to successful investing to sell your money-makers as close to their peak as you can; ideally just as you begin to see evidence of a slowdown in the sector. When the market starts to shift gears and move into reverse, call your broker even if everyone says the rally should continue for some time.

Unfortunately, those first signs are not all that easy to identify, even for professionals. The media, for example, only starts reporting on a recession when we're already in the middle of one. Long before the news is making headlines, the sector has already been affected and that is reflected in the stock price.

Here's a brief review of what is in store for each industry sub-sector.

Diamonds
Producers of these luxurious bits of gleaming carbon are some of the strongest long-term prospects in the resource sector, as there's every indication that diamonds will continue to command a high rate of return. As a luxury good, they don't go through the economic cycles that the other sub-sectors are known for. The market for diamonds is projected to increase for several years.

The downside of investing in diamond mining companies is that it's an expensive and risky business. It costs a fortune to dig for diamonds, and the odds of being successful are not good. And that's why the biggest timing factor in this sub-sector is investor fatigue— people simply run out of hope that they're going to see a return on their investment anytime soon, so they bail. Determine your level of risk before you invest, but consider this: if you own shares in a company that eventually finds some diamonds, then you're set.

Gold

When this precious metal started to boom in 2003, it hit US$400 per ounce, making it worthwhile for exploration teams to begin digging in earnest. Gold is tough to find (easier than diamonds, but still difficult) and production from existing mines isn't projected to meet market demand. Thus, the whole sector is dependent on explorers finding enough to satisfy global consumers. If interest rates stay low, then the price of gold is expected to keep on climbing, resulting in a boom that could last for years.

Metals

Base metals have been in a financial slump for decades, which has put a lid on exploration and mine development. The lack of activity has shrunk the inventories at metal-producing companies, in some cases, to a critical low. So as global demand for nickel and copper (two metals that are extremely sensitive to changes in the economy) increases, prices for these commodities will rise steadily.

Chronic shortages of nickel will likely be the norm for the next few years. Growing demand should then push the price of nickel up as long as inventories are diminishing. The boom will fizzle when inventories are rebuilt and demand is being met.

A key point to remember is that not all base metals operate on the same cycle. Take copper, for example. There's no shortage of copper, but the increased demand is still driving up commodity prices. As long as interest rates remain low, and countries continue to spend money on major infrastructure projects, then the shares of companies that produce base metals should rise on average for several years.

Oil and Gas

This volatile sector is known for its short cycles, which means that even though it might be a good time to sell shares in oil and gas producers, it won't be long before it's time to buy back in. In 2003, international drilling activity was at its highest level in five years. When the contents of the newly discovered reserves hit the market, demand will be satisfied, inventories will be rebuilt, and then prices will start to decline. Keep a close eye on this sector, because as prices drop, production gets cut back, inventories decline, and the next boom begins.

Coal

Using the rule of thumb that the best time to invest in any natural resource is when the situation in the sector and the outlook for the commodity are at their bleakest, then the timing is just about perfect to invest in coal producers. After years of mining more coal than the market needs, and burdened by ensuing glut, producers had to make sweeping changes in order to survive. The few companies that are still around are well-positioned to profit—they just need the world market for coal to heat up. That could happen, but it hinges on several factors, namely environmental concerns which could cool demand in North America. The only real potential for a sustained boom in this market is an increased demand from overseas consumers.

Uranium

Given the proliferation of nuclear power stations, the prospects for uranium producers are positively glowing. If demand continues at the current rate, then existing uranium inventories could be virtually eliminated in the near future. Considering that it takes a long time to discover uranium deposits and develop new mines, there could be a shortage of high-grade uranium unless the junior exploration companies unearth new reserves. If the new sources are low-grade, then they will be expensive to produce and process, a factor that could cause the price of uranium to rise over the next few years. Signs are that the boom in this sub-sector could continue for years.

Paper and Forestry Products

This industry has endured reams of bad luck in the last twenty years, resulting in share prices that are a bargain by any investment standards. Of course, they're cheap for a reason—the companies have been bleeding money for years. The good news is that they've managed to survive in a bad market for this long, so they only need a turnaround in pricing and demand for their products to pull them out of the slump. A booming economy should take care of this—the housing market is already doing its share.

Fertilizers

The last raging bull market for stocks in fertilizer producers began in 1993 and ended in 1996. Almost ten years later, the market remains relatively flat. The odds are strong that a rebound in the global economy will spark some growth in the market for fertilizers.

All in all, the resource sector is ready to boom for several years. As one sub-sector begins to peak, another gets ready to take off. Keep your eye on the timing of these cycles, and you'll profit from the next global boom in natural resources.

ACKNOWLEDGEMENTS

Many thanks to the team at Mavrix Funds for their support: Ray Steele, Bill Shaw, Sergio Di Vito, Craig Allardyce, Roger Dent, Mario Arra, Alex Nayyar, Aaron Friesen, Avnee Patel, Rahul Chawla, Durwin Pryce, Cecile Bannister, Shameeza Sherman, Sarah Fordham, Savio Fernandes, Harry Doniego, Paul Bruno, Dave Balsdon, Raluca Sarbu, Olivia Vo and especially to Mark Riedl, Paul Miklasevics, Carrie Parris and Donnette Markland for the extra help that made the book possible.

Special thanks to numerous people in the investment industry for providing data, comments, charts, insights, and more including: David Christie of TD Securities; Corey Hammill of Paradigm Capital; Don Poirier of First Associates; Eric Zaunscherb of Raymond James; Johann Aler and Ian Howat of NB Financial; Pierre Lacroix and Richard Kelertas of Desjardins Securities; David Talbot and Bob Boaz of Dundee Securities; Jacob Bout of CIBC; John Hughes, Cristina Rossi and Gareth Watson of Scotia Capital; and Mike Padley at Peters and Co.

There are many geologists, prospectors and entrepreneurs that I'd like to thank for making this sector such a dynamic one to track, but that list is too long to include here. Thanks to those who agreed to be interviewed for the book, namely: Randy Turner of Diamondex Resources; Kerry Curtis of Cumberland Resources; Geoff Chater of First Quantum; and Charles Reid of Canfor.

A note of thanks to veteran journalists Gordon Pitts and Andrew Allentuck for not discouraging this money manager from attempting to write a book.

Most of all, thanks to my wonderful family—Laila, Skai, Eric and Sandra who tolerated my working on this book during our family holiday, weekends and evenings.

Mal Spooner, Toronto, December 2003

ACKNOWLEDGEMENTS

Shakespeare wrote: "All the world's a stage / And all the men and women merely players." Mal is one of the most dynamic players that I've had the honor of working with. We met in 1986 when I joined the editorial staff of Benefits Canada. The editor, John Milne, insisted if I had any questions about pension fund investments that I shouldn't hesitate to call one of the board members, Mal Spooner. John was right—Mal's answers were always straightforward, and most refreshingly, delivered with a wicked sense of humour.

A few years later, I moved to Hungary and while working there as a freelance business journalist, recalled many of the insights Mal had shared on the workings of markets and economies. I returned to Canada in the mid 1990s and switched to reporting on health care. When Mal approached me with the idea of writing a book on investing in Canadian resources, I suggested that he enlist the services of an investment writer as I hadn't covered the industry in years. Being a contrarian, he grinned, and said: "Perfect."

Our collaboration on writing this book has been a successful one. I fired off the questions that I—a neophyte investor with a genuine aversion to "risky" resource stocks—wanted answers to. His replies were succinct and, despite being laced with investment vernacular, easy to understand. So thanks, Mal, it's been a great learning experience.

I'd also like to thank Susan Gural for helping with the research; Mark Riedl for answering lots of questions with patience and a smile; and Carrie Parris and Donnette Markland for all of their administrative wizardry. Numerous other people have also been a tremendous support, especially Michael Collins, Freda Dong, Eric Gerritsen and Mary McGugan.

Thanks to my family: Dyliss, Arlene, Glenn and Deb, Harvey, Eva, Rob and Paula. I'd like to dedicate my work to my father, Gordon Clarke, as he was the best investment advisor and mentor that I've ever had.

Above all, I'm very grateful to my incredibly supportive husband, Tom, and my children, Rebecca and Daniel.

Pamela Clarke, North Vancouver, December 2003

INDEX

2001 Goldcorp Challenge, 56, 153

Aber Diamond Corp., 37, 39, 46, 143, 146
Aber Resources Ltd., 39, 146
Abitibi-Consolidated Inc., 33, 105, 109, 185
Acclaim Energy Trust, 89, 173
Afghanistan, 27, 54
Africa, 25, 60-61, 73, 86, 92, 113, 115,
    154, 157-158, 161-162, 165, 170
Agrium Inc., 115-117, 183
Ainsworth Lumber Co., 109
Alaska, 155, 157
Alberta, 41, 43, 89, 115, 120, 131, 133,
    169, 171, 173, 175-176, 178, 181-182,
    186
Alcan Inc., 72, 73, 158
Alcoa, 72
Algeria, 81, 174, 177
Allaire, Steven A., 175
Alley, Kenneth, 176
Aluminum, 72, 158
Anglo Gold, 58
Argentina, 33, 61, 115-116, 148, 154, 156,
    183
Argyle Mine, 45
Assie, George B., 179
Athabasca Basin, Saskatchewan, 100
Aur Resources Inc., 30, 159
Australia, 25, 33, 45, 50, 92, 97, 99-100,
    114-115, 133, 148, 157-158, 164-165,
    167
Automobile industry, 67
    producers, 66
    sales, 66, 67, 93

B.C. (British Columbia), 17, 43, 59, 120,
    144-146, 150-151, 157, 160, 162, 166-
    167, 175, 180-181, 186, 190, 192
BHP Billiton Diamonds Inc., 39, 46, 145
BMW, 67
Bahamas, 134
Baldwin, Douglas D., 177
Barbados, 161, 171
Barrick Gold Corp., 30, 33, 56, 58, 148

Base metals, 21, 43, 52, 65-73, 75-77,
    168, 196
    exploration, 60
    mining, 29
    producers, 67, 76
Belzile, Andre, 187
Bema Gold Corp., 61
Bentley, Peter J.G., 186
Biemans, Roger, 171
Blusson, Stewart, 39, 47
Boiler-room set-ups, 137
Boivin, Claude, 191
Boland, Brad, 153
Bolivar Gold Corp., 61
Botswana, 40, 42, 165
Boxboard, 108, 187
Boyd, Sean, 147
Brazil, 108, 115, 151, 154-155, 158, 160-
    161, 164, 167, 171, 184
Bre-X Minerals Ltd., 16, 19, 34, 131-137
Brenneman, Ron A., 174
Brown, Maynard E., 145
Brownlee, Wayne R., 184
Buchan, Robert M., 155
Buckee, James W., 177

Caldwell, Scott A., 155
Calgary, Alberta, 31, 169-178, 181, 183
Calpine Corp., 89
Cambior Inc., 149
Cameco Corp., 99-100, 179-180
Canadian equity market, 103
Canadian Forest Products, 105, 186
Canadian Natural Resources Ltd., 30, 83,
    170
Canadian Occidental Petroleum Ltd., 86
Canadian softwood, 105
Canfor Corp., 105, 109, 186
Canico Resource Corp., 160
Capital gains tax, 123
Carbon dioxide emissions, 94-95
Carlin Trend, Nevada, 33
Carrington, John K., 148
Carroll, Michael L., 150

Cascades Inc., 187
Case Alcan Inc., 72
Cayman Islands, 134
Cequel Energy Inc., 88
Chad, 171
Chernobyl, 97-98
Chile, 30, 33, 148, 155-157, 159, 161, 167, 184, 191
China, 23-25, 28, 44, 61, 67, 83, 92, 94-95, 99, 108, 113-117, 158, 172, 185
Chislett, Albert, 130
Clarke, Gordon, 200
The Club of Rome, 80
Coal, 13, 21, 82, 91-95, 111, 167, 181-182, 197
    coking coal, 93-94
    industry, 93
    mining, 94
    producers, 91-93, 95, 197
Collins, Michael, 200
Colombia, 177
Colt, Edward H., 156
Cominco Ltd., 72, 93, 115, 167
Conway, Joseph F., 154
Copper, 27, 34, 37, 52, 60, 65-66, 68, 70-75, 130-132, 157, 159, 161-164, 166-167, 196
    prices, 34, 70, 72
    smelting, 74
Costigan, Gerald R., 178
Crude oil, 81-83, 169, 173, 175-176
Cuba, 182
Cumberland Resources Ltd., 60, 150
    Meadowbank Mine, 62, 150
Curtis, Kerry, 60, 150
Cypress Energy, 88
Cyprus Amax Minerals Co., 74
Czech Republic, 158

DaimlerChrysler, 67
Daughney, V. Edward, 192
Dawson, Scott, 178
Day, Nicholas, 91
De Beers, 39-40, 43, 144
Delaney, Ian W., 182
Democratic Republic of Congo, 74, 162
Denmark, 174

Dia Met Minerals Ltd., 39
Diammonium phosphate, 113
Diamond, 13, 16, 30, 37-48, 55, 59-60, 65, 86, 99, 111, 123, 130-131, 141, 143-146, 154, 195-196
    blood-free, 42, 45-46
    Canadian diamonds, 39, 42, 44-45
    companies, 41, 46, 48, 143
    diamondiferous kimberlite, 45
    exploration, 43, 60, 99
    industry, 40-41, 44, 46
    kimberlite, 38-39, 45, 47-48
    non-diamondiferous kimberlite, 38
    producers, 45, 143
Diamond Field Resources, 130
Diamondex Resources Ltd., 39, 43, 144
Diamonds North Resources Ltd., 43, 145
Diavik Mine, Northwest Territories, 39-40, 42, 46, 143, 146, 154
Dietz, James F., 184
Dominican Republic, 161
Domtar Inc., 106, 188
Dong, Freda, 200
Doolan, Michael, 161
Dottori, Frank A., 191
Douglas, Jon A., 166
Downie, Ewan S., 168
Doyle, William J., 184
Drouin, Richard, 185
Dubé, Christian, 188
Dumas, Michel, 191
Dundee Securities, 51, 58
Dynatec, 76

Echo Bay Mines Ltd., 63, 155
Eckhardt, Ron J., 177
Ecuador, 154, 171
Edey, Grant A., 154
Ekati Mine, Northwest Territories, 39-40, 42, 46
Eldorado Gold Corp., 61, 151
Eldorado Nuclear Ltd., 99
Elk Valley Coal, 93
Emerson, David L., 186
Encal Energy, 89, 175
EnCana Corp., 83, 171
Energy companies, 32, 79, 84, 169

cycle, 90
   stocks, 22, 83, 85
   trust, 87-89, 173
Engen, Travis, 158
Environmental hurdles, 21, 60
Environmental wild card, 95
Environmentalists, 80, 98
Eresman, Randy, 171

Falconbridge Ltd., 30, 33, 69, 71-72, 130, 161
Farrow, Catharine, 163
Felderhof, John, 131
Fertilizer, 13, 111-117, 182-184, 193, 198
   companies, 112-113, 183
   industries, 193
   market, 115-116
   phosphate fertilizer, 113-114
   producers, 114, 116, 198
Fipke, Chuck, 39, 47, 123
First Quantum Minerals Ltd., 73-75, 162
Ford Motor Co., 67
Fortier, Yves, 158
France, 24, 98, 158, 187-188, 191
Friedland, Robert, 129

Gagel, Ronald P., 159
Gagnon, Charles, 191
Gammiero, Dominic, 189
Gannicott, Bob, 37, 143
Gardiner, Jim G., 181
Garofalo, David, 147
Gas, 13, 21-22, 31-32, 41, 79-90, 94, 101-102, 111-112, 114, 116, 120, 122, 169-178, 182, 193, 196
General Motors Corp., 67
George, Rick, 176
Georgia-Pacific, 106
Germany, 24, 158, 174, 187
Gerritsen, Eric, 200
Ghana, 154
Gignac, Louis P., 149
Gill, James W., 159
Girard, Jacques, 188
Glamis Gold Ltd., 152
Gold exploration, 33, 56
   explorers, 55

industry, 53, 153
   mining, 47, 55, 58, 61, 99, 157
   producers, 33, 52, 57-58, 60, 71, 147-148, 154-155, 179
Goldcorp Inc., 30, 55-56, 62, 153
Grandey, Gerald W., 179
Grandin, Michael A., 181
Greenspan, Allan, 25-26, 53
Groundwood paper manufacturer, 185
Guatemala, 152

Hakimi, Farokh S., 164
Hames, Marilyn P.A., 157
Hand, Scott M., 164
Harke, Caroline, 144
Hislop, Barbara R., 186
Honda, 67
Honduras, 152
Humphrey, Bruce, 153
Hungary, 158, 200
Husky Energy Inc., 172
Hyundai Motor Co., 67

Iamgold Corp., 61, 154
Iceland, 158
Idaho, 156
Imperial Oil Ltd., 83
Inco Ltd., 30, 33, 68-69, 71, 75, 130, 160, 163-164
India, 23-25, 28, 44, 92, 94, 114, 158
Indonesia, 81, 132-133, 164, 177
Intel Corp., 26
Iran, 81
Iraq, 22, 27, 54, 81, 108
Iraq War, 81, 108
Ireland, 158
Iron ore, 66

Jakarta, Indonesia, 132
Japan, 24, 98, 161
Jeannes, Charles A., 152
Jewelry industry, 52
   market, 38
   producers, 46
Johannesburg, South Africa, 50
Johnson, David D., 175
Jones, Peter C., 164

Kahlert, Bernard, 145
Kakfwi, Stephen, 41
Kazakhstan, 30, 158, 174
Keevil, Norman B., 167
Kelowna, B.C., 190
Kemess Mines, B.C., 59-60, 62, 166
Kennecott Canada Exploration, 39
Kennedy, Brian J., 156
Kenyon, Michael, 160
Kerr, David W., 161
Kerr, Hamish, 192
Ketch Resources Ltd., 89, 173
Kinross Gold Corp., 63, 155
Kisladag, Turkey, 151
Klaproth, Martin, 98
Klondike Gold Rush, 19
Knowles, Henry J., 168
Kolebaba, Mark, 145
Korea, 24, 158, 185
Kraft, 186
Kuwait, 81
Kyrgyzstan, 99, 179

Labrador, 75, 130, 164
Langille, John G., 170
Lau, John C.S., 172
Laut, Steve W., 170
Lemaire, Alain, 187
Lemaire, Bernard, 187
Lemaire, Laurent, 187
Lewanski, Richard, 169
Libya, 81, 174
LionOre Mining International Ltd., 165
Long Penn West, 89
Lough, James C., 169
Luscar Ltd., 93
Lyons, Terry, 59, 166

MacGibbon, Terry, 75, 163
MacMillan Bloedel Ltd., 17
Maher, Cheryl S., 152
Majescor Resources, 43
Malaysia, 158, 177
Mali, 154
Manitoba, 120, 155, 159, 168

Marginal tax, 119, 122-123
Markin, Allan P., 170
Martin, Bert, 189
Maschmeyer, Dennis G., 182
Mayers, Theodore C., 165
McArthur, C. Kevin, 152
McCarter, Peter N., 159
McDonald, John, 144
McDonald, Michael D., 177
McElligott, Paul J., 192
McEwen, Rob, 55, 153
McGee, Neil D., 172
McGugan, Mary, 200
McIntyre, Norman I., 174
McLennan, Rex J., 157
McLeod, Bruce, 146
McLeod-Seltzer, Catherine, 146
Meridian Gold Inc., 60, 156
Merszei, Geoffrey, 158
Metcalfe, Darryl, 173
Mexico, 93, 152, 156, 167, 187-188
Milne, John, 200
Mkubwa, Bwana, 74
Mongolia, 99, 179
Montreal, Quebec, 158, 185, 188, 191
Moody's Investors Service, 103
Moore, Michael, 190
Morgan, Gwyn, 171
Munk, Peter, 33, 56, 148
Murphy, Alice, 143

Namibia, 167
National Energy Program, 32, 41
Natural gas, 22, 80, 82-83, 94, 112, 114,
    116, 169-171, 173, 175-177, 193
Netherlands, 158, 174, 182
Nevada, 33, 50, 56, 60, 148, 152, 155-156
New Brunswick, 119
New Caledonia, 69, 161, 164
New York, 26, 44
Newall, Clive, 74, 162
Newfoundland, 68, 119, 156, 159, 164
Newmont Mining Corp., 58
Newsprint, 102-103, 107-109, 185, 191
Nexen Inc., 83, 86
Nexfor Inc., 109, 189
Nickel, 27, 43, 52, 65-66, 68-72, 94, 130-

131, 160-161, 163-165, 182, 196
   laterite class, 160
   producers, 69, 71
Nigeria, 81
Nikiforuk, Steve, 173
Nitrogen, 112, 114, 116, 183-184
Nitrogen fertilizer, 112, 114, 116
   gas, 112
   industry, 114
Norske Skog Canada Ltd., 109
North Sea, 86, 170
Northern Telecom, 16
Northgate Exploration Ltd., 59-60, 62, 166
Northwest Territories, 39, 41, 43, 120,
   123, 143-146, 154, 166
Nova Scotia, 119
Nuclear energy, 97
   fission, 98
   power, 82, 98-100, 197
   power industry, 98
   power stations, 99-100, 197
   reactors, 97-99
Nunavut, 40-41, 43, 60, 120, 131, 144-
   146, 150, 155, 168
Nusamba, 134

OPEC, (Organization of Petroleum
   Exporting Countries) 81-82, 84
Oil, 13, 21-22, 28, 30-33, 41, 79-90, 92, 94,
   101-102, 111, 122, 133, 169-178, 182,
   196
Oliver, John E., 155
Onça-Puma, 160
Ontario, 55, 99, 119, 123, 131, 134-135,
   153, 155, 159, 163-164, 168, 176, 179,
   182, 185

Panama, 159
PanCanadian Energy Corp., 171
Paper products, 106, 108-109, 187
Papua New Guinea, 157
Park, Beverlee, 192
Pascall, Philip, 74, 162
Penn West Petroleum, 89
Penner, Douglas N., 178
Penny, Brian W., 155
Peru, 33, 148-149, 156, 164, 167

Petro-Canada Ltd., 30, 33, 174
Peugeot-Citroën, 67
Philpot, Michael O., 162
Placer Dome Inc., 30, 58, 157
Plywood, 104, 109, 190
Point Lake, Northwest Territories, 39
Popowich, Jim L., 181
Potash, 113, 116-117, 183-184
Potash Corp. of Saskatchewan, 116-117,
   184
Potassium, 112-113
Price, Earl W., 151
PrimeWest Energy Trust, 88
Prince Edward Island, 119
Progress Energy Ltd., 89, 175
Proll, Douglas A., 170
Puerto Rico, 158
Pugliese, William D., 154
Pulp inventories, 108
   producers, 186

Qatar, 81, 171, 177

Red Lake, Ontario, 55, 62, 153
Regent, Aaron W., 161
Reid, Charles, 186
Renault-Nissan, 67
Riverside Forest Products Ltd., 190
Roberts, Harry, 174
Robins, John, 146
Rogers, Terry V., 179
Romania, 61
Ross, John C., 163
Rougeau, Pierre, 185
Rowley, Martin R., 162
Royalty trusts, 86-89
Royer, Raymond, 188
Russia, 24, 30, 40, 42, 45, 61, 83, 92, 108,
   113, 115, 155, 161

Saskatchewan, 40, 97, 99-100, 116, 120,
   153, 179-180, 184
Saudi Arabia, 81-82
Scherkus, Ebe, 147
Seaman, John, 168
Senegal, 154
September 11, 26, 44

Shell Canada Ltd., 83
Sherritt International Corp., 94, 182
Shineton, J. Barrie, 189
Shklanka, Roman, 160
Sierra Leone, 30
Simpson, Yale, 145
Slovenia, 158
Smith, Adam, 80
Smith, Tony, 173
Snap Lake Mine, Northwest Territories,
   39-40, 42, 144
Softwood lumber, 110, 186
   plywood, 190
   saga, 105
Sokalsky, Jamie C., 148
Sorensen, Stephen, 180
South Africa, 92, 154, 157, 161
South America, 25, 60, 159
South Dakota, 153
South Korea, 24, 185
Southern Cross Resources Inc., 99
Southwestern Resources Corp., 61
Spain, 24, 158, 182
Stainless steel, 68
Stanyer, Warren, 180
Steel industry, 93
Steele, Gordon, 190
Stewart, John M., 175
Steyn, Colin H., 165
Stockford, Howard R., 159
Stowe, Ken, 59, 166
Sudan, 30, 86, 177
Sudbury, Ontario, 75, 163
Suncor Energy Inc., 83, 176
Sweden, 187
Sweeney, Paul B., 160
Swift, Lloyd C., 169
Switzerland, 24, 158
Syria, 174

T-bills, 53
Taiwan, 109
Talisman Energy Inc., 30, 83, 86, 177
Tanzania, 33, 148, 157
Tax advantages, 87
   deductible investments, 120
   haven, 134

Taylor, Jay K., 157
Taylor, John G., 167
Tech bubble, 24-26, 35, 68, 136
Teck Cominco Ltd., 72, 93, 115, 145, 167
Tembec Inc., 103, 105, 109, 191
Tempest Energy Corp., 178
Thailand, 117, 158, 185
Thiele, Brad G., 150
Thomas, Eira, 146
Thomas, Grenville, 47
Thompson, David A., 167
Thompson, John F.H., 167
TimberWest Forest Corp., 192
Trinidad and Tobago, 174, 177, 184
Toronto, Ontario, 17, 39, 43, 134, 143,
   147-148, 153-155, 159, 161, 163-165,
   168, 182, 189
Toyota Motor Co., 67
Tremayne, John, 189
Tunisia, 174
Turkey, 61, 151, 158, 164, 167
Turner, Randy, 39, 47, 144

U.K., (United Kingdom), 28, 44, 51, 187
U.S. Geological Survey, 68
U.S. Housing Starts, 104
Ukraine, 97, 115
Union Camp Corp., 106
United Arab Emirates, 81, 171
Uranium, 13, 97-100, 111, 179-180, 197
   exploration, 100
   inventories, 99, 197
   mining properties, 99
   producers, 99, 197

Vancouver, B.C., 39, 43, 45, 144-146, 150-
   151, 157, 160, 162, 166-167, 180, 186,
   192, 200
Venezuela, 61, 81, 174
Verbiski, Chris, 130
Vézina, Raynald, 149
Voisey's Bay, Newfoundland and
   Labrador, 68, 130-131, 136, 164
Voorhees, James S., 152

Walsh, David, 131, 133
Wanner, Kirby, 173